Making a Drama out of a Crisis

Resources available for download

A playscript for Aladdin is available online at
www.continuumbooks.com/resources/9781855394469.

Please visit the link and register with us to receive your password and
access to these downloadable resources.

If you experience any problems accessing the resources, please contact
Continuum at info@continuumbooks.com

Also available from Network Continuum

With Drama in Mind – Patrice Baldwin

Challenging Behaviour – Anne Copley

Available from Continuum

Getting the Buggers to Behave, 3rd Edition – Sue Cowley

Making a Drama out of a Crisis

Improving classroom behaviour through drama techniques and exercises

Tommy Donbavand

network
continuum

For Anne Swarbrick
the drama teacher who encouraged me
to pursue a career in the theatre

Continuum International Publishing Group
Network Continuum
The Tower Building   80 Maiden Lane, Suite 704
11 York Road   New York,
SE1 7NX   NY 10038

www.networkcontinuum.co.uk
www.continuumbooks.com

British Library Cataloguing-in-Publication Data
A catalogue record for this book is available from the British Library.

ISBN: 9781855394469 (paperback)

Library of Congress Cataloging-in-Publication Data
A catalog record for this book is available from the Library of Congress

Typeset by Ben Cracknell
Printed and bound in Great Britain by MPG Books Ltd , Bodmin, Cornwall

Contents

Contact

The days of books being a one-way experience are coming to an end; thanks to email and the internet, authors now have direct contact with their readers.

If there is anything you'd like to discuss with me about the activities and exercises contained in this book, to learn more about my other writing projects, or simply to say hello and tell me how drama works in your classroom, please visit my website at:

www.tommydonbavand.com

Or, you can email me at:

drama@tommydonbavand.com

I frequently visit schools to run creative writing and drama workshops, encourage reading through fun activities, and talk about life as an author. If this is something you think would benefit your pupils, please contact me at the above address.

Introduction

Children never misbehave

How does that sentence make you feel? Surprised? Bewildered? Angry? If you're a teacher, your response is likely to be a mixture of all three – especially if you've just come home from a class that's run you ragged all day and you've opened this book in the hope of finding a solution to dealing with the little horrors.

I'm going to stick to my opinion, though: children never *mis*behave – they merely behave in the manner that is most attractive to them at that moment. It could be that they're testing the boundaries of the teacher/pupil relationship, or that they're out to try and impress their friends. They may be making a mistake, or be fully aware they should not be doing what they are about to do. Their classmates may be egging them on, or they may be acting completely alone. Whatever they're doing, it is all a way of behaving – and any type of behaviour can be modified.

Now, if you're hoping for an academic tome that peers into pupils' minds and tells you the social, environmental and psychological reasons for the way they act, I'm sorry to tell you that you've picked up the wrong book. Don't crease the spine and you may be able to get a refund . . .

This book simply provides tried and tested methods for improving your pupils' behaviour through drama activities and exercises. Methods that work.

Why drama?

We all crave a little drama in our lives and, whether you get yours from a popular TV soap opera, a gripping novel or a trip to the theatre – it fulfils the same need that mankind has experienced for centuries. We see it in cave paintings, hear it in stories passed down through generations of churchgoers, and experience it from actors who started out as street players, treated no better than thieves or beggars. Drama is a necessity, not a luxury.

Yet, with the curriculum becoming focused more and more on academic success, drama is starting to disappear from our children's education. Thanks to a number of dedicated teachers, the subject has not yet disappeared (you may even *be* one of those teachers), but it is climbing the endangered lessons list quickly.

The situation, however, isn't entirely bleak. Your pupils still get a daily dose of drama from TV screens, computer games and even the odd book – but their participation is limited to that of an audience member, a distant viewer. They don't get to take part in the drama – and that is exactly why it works when helping to improve the behavioural choices they make. It's all new to them.

Drama is a great leveller; anyone can take part regardless of age, academic ability or physical handicap. There are no rights or wrongs in the subject – just choices. It's these choices that determine what your pupils get in return for their efforts – just like the choices they make in their behaviour.

What can drama do for me?

This book is split into two halves – the first packed with quick and easy drama-based games, exercises and activities that you can run with little or no preparation. These exercises are split into chapters that cover topics such as helping your pupils to pay attention, ways to stop them chatting in class, and even ideas for dealing with inappropriate language.

The second half of the book features a major project that will enable the entire class to work together, leaving no one out. I'll be telling you how to stage a pantomime with your pupils (there's even a complete *Aladdin* script for you to adapt to your own needs) – a project that everyone can get involved with, no matter what their interests or abilities.

The book is designed so that you can read from start to finish, or dip in and out to a subject that's important to you. You'll find that some of the exercises cover the same topic from a slightly different angle, and you may discover that you have ideas of how to alter or change the activities to better suit your situation. Please go right ahead and do just that. It would be impossible for me to anticipate every pupil in every school and create something that would help each one individually – so take these ideas as a starting point and adapt them however you wish.

As much as possible, these exercises and activities have been tested in real-life classrooms, either by myself in my capacity as a workshop leader, or by one of several teachers who offered to give the ideas a trial run. If any of the exercises failed (i.e. they were of no help whatsoever) they were cut from the book. However, in practice, that rarely happened, as what did nothing for one class sometimes worked wonders with another.

With this in mind, you may draw a complete blank with some of the activities. You may run them to a sea of disinterested faces. Don't worry – just pick another exercise and give that a go. You'll soon find something that works for your pupils.

Who do you think you are?

At this very moment, some of you reading this book are thinking these exact words. Who does this guy think he is, and what gives him the right to tell me how to control my classroom?

Simply put, I don't have that right. I've never worked as a full-time teacher, and I don't have a handful of letters after my name to prove I've spent years studying what makes young people tick. I do, however, know how drama can affect children.

I studied drama and English with passion at school and announced to the world fairly early on that I wanted to be an actor. I found myself faced with the usual response of 'Yes, but what are you *really* going to do?' from all but three people – my parents and my drama teacher.

At 16, I went to college to take a drama foundation course alongside my A levels, intent that I was going to be a serious, Shakespearean actor. However, things didn't go exactly as I planned them and, when I left at 18, I found myself working with children on the Isle of Wight – as a clown.

I'd taught myself a little basic magic and balloon modelling in order to entertain at local birthday parties while I studied the 'serious' side of the stage, little knowing that this would be the direction my career would finally take. I entertained at holiday centres around the UK for the next few years, incorporating what I had learned at drama school as often as I could, and always with great success.

I then took to the sea as children's entertainer on board a cruise liner, soon rising to the lofty position of entertainments manager. I was now responsible for arranging the day-to-day activities for over 700 people, while writing and producing shows for their evening entertainment. Again, the drama training was invaluable.

I came back to dry land when I was offered the chance to audition for a musical in London's West End. The show was *Buddy: The Buddy Holly Story*, and the role I won was that of the MC at Buddy's final concert in Clearlake, Iowa. Straight after this show, Buddy boarded a plane with The Big Bopper and Ritchie Valens for a short-lived flight into the history books.

I stayed with *Buddy* for eight years, including brief stints on the UK tour and Toronto productions. While in the show, I began to assemble and write up the dozens of activities and games I had invented over my years as a children's entertainer and wrote a book – *Quick Fixes For Bored Kids* – which was published in 2001 by How To Books. Three further titles followed and I was soon visiting schools and appearing on radio shows up and down the country, to talk about the tricky subject of keeping kids entertained.

As a result of this, I was asked by the Society of London Theatre to prepare and run a drama workshop for their forthcoming Kids Week. The workshop explored the life of Buddy Holly and the impact he had on both rock 'n' roll and popular music. Once again, I was reminded of the immense teaching power of drama. I was soon asked to repeat the exercise for popular Queen musical, *We Will Rock You*.

When *Buddy* closed in 2002, I joined the production team of a children's theatre company where I wrote, directed and appeared in dozens of productions which toured both schools and theatres. All of these shows were interactive, fun and used drama as a way to explain or teach a topic. I knew I was onto something . . .

I then set myself up as a freelance author, writing five titles in Egmont Books' *Too Ghoul For School* series, several episodes of the hit Children's BBC TV show *Planet Cook*, and creating my series of comedy horror novels, *Scream Street*. I also wrote dozens of articles for magazines such as *The Times Educational Supplement*, *Junior Education* and *Practical Professional Child Care*.

Finally, I was in a position to pitch a book that explored the use of drama as both an educational and social tool. The book you now have in your hands.

If you'd like to contact me concerning anything in this book, you can do so through my website at www.tommydonbavand.com.

To the point

Now that I'm able to share my experience in using drama with children, I should also let you into another secret – a trick that has saved me countless problems over the years and can be used as a way to reward and discourage behavioural choices in any situation. Give out points.

It really is as simple as that. If you install a points system in your classroom, you'll discover that you can award and remove points for good work and unwelcome behaviour. So long as you make these points count for something (such as the chance to watch a movie in class if a specific number of points are earned by the end of the month), pupils will treat them as though they are made of solid gold.

I started using points systems as I didn't want to be constantly handing out prizes to the children who 'won' my games, nor did I want any of them to be 'out' and have to sit on the sidelines bored as a game progressed. So, I started awarding points for how successful each participant was in a particular activity – ten points for doing your best, eight for trying really hard, six for giving the activity a go, and so on. I also discovered that, if I themed the points system, it was even more of a success. For example, while on the cruise liner I renamed the points to doubloons – and the kids worked harder than ever to earn them!

All you need to do is provide each child with a notebook they can carry around school, in which you mark the number of points they have earned for a specific game or activity. You can simply keep track of the points on a wall chart but, in my experience, children like to be able to take their books home to show their parents just how well they are doing.

Now, decide whether you're going to be awarding points, doubloons, stars, diamonds – or anything else you think your pupils will respond to winning. You'll be marking their books in exactly the same way, but the fact that the points are called something special will help a great deal.

Finally, explain the way the points system works. From now on, you will be awarding points for good work, and deducting them for anyone who breaks the rules (you can either restrict the system to the drama exercises in this book, or extend it to each of your lessons – the choice is yours).

Give your pupils a group target to reach. Perhaps if they earn a total of a thousand points in a week, they get an extra hour of Golden Time or, as in the example above, five thousand points wins the chance to watch a DVD. And before you complain that you'll have to add up thousands of points each week, simply ask your pupils to swap books with someone else and add up the totals, checking just one or two books yourself. If they think you'll subtract 500 points for cheating, your class's maths skills will suddenly be perfect!

Get more help

Of course, there will be times when all the drama exercises or points in the world won't stop certain pupils from acting up and, sooner or later, you'll have to face the possibility that there is something other than inappropriate behavioural choices happening.

Now, I'm the first to raise my hand and admit that I am not an expert in problems such as ADHD, dyspraxia and Asperger's syndrome. I do have some experience with children who have learning difficulties, both through my drama work and in the fact that my stepson suffers from Developmental Coordination Disorder. I urge you to speak to a medical professional if you suspect that a child in your class or school is in need of specialist help.

However, I have done some research into what to look out for in such a situation. The following lists of potential symptoms are not exhaustive, nor does every sufferer display them in the same way – but they may help you to spot a child whose behaviour warrants additional care.

Attention Deficit Hyperactivity Disorder (ADHD)

Pupils that just used to be labelled as hyperactive or unruly are now being diagnosed with ADHD or its cousin, ADD (Attention Deficit Disorder). The symptoms are varied and may not all be present in all sufferers, but may include:

- A very short attention span
- Being very easily distracted
- Being unable to stick at tasks that are tedious, or time consuming
- Being unable to listen to, or carry out, instructions
- Being unable to concentrate, and constantly changing activity, or task
- Being unable to sit still, especially in calm or quiet surroundings
- Constantly fidgeting
- Being unable to settle to tasks
- Excessive physical movement
- Being unable to wait for a turn
- Acting without thinking
- Breaking any set rules
- Little or no sense of danger.

(NHS Direct website:
www.nhsdirect.nhs.uk/articles/article.aspx?articleId=40&sectionId=10)

If you suspect that one of your pupils is acting in this way, please speak to your school nurse or headteacher to set in motion the arrangements for help. Further information can be found at the website of Attention Deficit Disorder Information and Support Service (ADDiSS): www.addiss.co.uk.

Developmental Coordination Disorder

DCD is a disorder linked to dyspraxia. Children with DCD have poor muscle development, motor skills and concentration – problems which can sometimes lead to inappropriate behaviour. Symptoms include:

- Very high levels of motor activity, including feet swinging and tapping when seated
- High levels of excitability, with a loud/shrill voice
- May be easily distressed and prone to temper tantrums
- May constantly bump into objects and fall over
- Hands flap when running
- Lack of any sense of danger: jumping from heights, etc.
- Avoidance of constructional toys, such as jigsaws or building blocks
- Poor fine motor skills: difficulty in holding a pencil or using scissors
- Lack of imaginative play
- Laterality (left- or right-handedness) still not established
- Persistent language difficulties
- Sensitive to sensory stimulation, including high levels of noise, tactile defensiveness
- Limited response to verbal instruction
- Limited concentration: tasks are often left unfinished
- Difficulties in adapting to a structured school routine
- Difficulties in physical education lessons
- Slow at dressing, including inability to tie shoelaces
- Barely legible handwriting
- Immature drawing and copying skills
- Literal use of language
- Inability to remember more than two or three instructions at once
- Slow completion of class work
- Tendency to become easily distressed and emotional.

(Dyspraxia Foundation website:
www.dyspraxiafoundation.org.uk/services/gu_symptoms.php)

As with ADHD, if you suspect that one of your pupils may be suffering from Developmental Coordination Disorder, seek professional help.

More information can be found on the website of the Dyspraxia Foundation: www.dyspraxiafoundation.org.uk.

Asperger's syndrome

A form of autism, Asperger's syndrome affects many children across the UK. Symptoms may include, but not be limited to:

- Being a loner
- Being aloof or passive
- Poor or exaggerated eye contact
- Lack of empathy
- Naivety
- Difficulty with group work in a classroom or in team sports like football
- Unable to initiate small talk
- Literal understanding of language
- Idiosyncratic language
- A love of routine with extreme distress if it changes
- Unusual play patterns, e.g. lining toys up or taking them apart
- Tendency to read factual rather than fiction books
- Clumsy
- Poor coordination, e.g. catching a ball or being accident prone
- Flapping movements or nervous tics
- May walk with a lumbering stooped gait.

(Asperger East Anglia website:
www.asperger.org.uk/thesyndrome/symptoms.htm)

As ever, please seek medical and/or professional help for advice on how to proceed if you suspect you may have a sufferer in your class. More information can be found from the Asperger's Syndrome Foundation: www.aspergerfoundation.org.uk.

Of course, these are not the only illnesses which could affect or modify the behaviour of one or more of your pupils. If you suspect that a child in your class may need help, talk to someone today.

I should also stress that, even if you have a sufferer in your class, they will still be able to enjoy and benefit from the drama exercises that follow. So, let's turn the page and get started . . .

Part One
GAMES AND ACTIVITIES TO IMPROVE BEHAVIOUR

1 Chatterboxes

Talk is cheap (or so the saying goes), but it can also be distracting. While effective communication is to be encouraged in the classroom, there are times when you just need your pupils to, well . . . shut up and listen.

The exercises that follow are designed to help bring silence into your classroom so that everyone can concentrate and, with any luck, learn. They're a mixture of activities and games that will grab your pupils' attention and take control of their mouths long enough for you to replace their own topics of conversation with whatever you want them to say and do.

Some of these exercises require a little forward planning or even a prop to be constructed beforehand – but the results will be well worth the effort and, before long, you'll be able to switch on the silence with a click of your fingers.

Don't forget that any of the ideas in this chapter can be adapted to suit your exact requirements; if you can think of a better way to run a particular exercise – go for it! You may even find that some of the ideas can be combined or tweaked to fit in with your current classes.

Now, let's get some peace and quiet . . .

Where in the world?

You'll need to prepare your pupils in advance for this exercise – but, don't worry . . . They won't know you're planning to commandeer their conversations, and they might even enjoy learning the snippets you'll have to offer.

All you have to do is pick a country that speaks another language. Perhaps your class or year group are already studying a foreign land and customs. If so, this exercise will be an ideal add-on to those lessons.

Let's say, for argument's sake, that you choose Germany as your country. Now, you need to teach your pupils a few words and phrases in German, such as these shown here:

Good morning – Guten Morgen

Good afternoon/day – Guten Tag

Good night – Gute Nacht

Excuse me – Entschuldigen Sie, bitte

Do you speak German? – Sprechen Sie Deutsch?

I speak a little German – Ich spreche ein bißchen Deutsch

Thank you very much – Vielen Dank

You're welcome – Bitte

Now, when your pupils are chattering and you want them to listen to you, all you have to do is display a German flag (you could pin one up, show it on the whiteboard or – if you're feeling adventurous – make a flagpole and hoist one up above your desk). As soon as the flag appears, they have to continue their chatter, but switch languages to the one shown.

Of course, the chance of your pupils being fluent in this new language is slim so, once their selection of phrases is used up, you should be able to quieten the classroom down and extinguish the conversations.

There is a possibility that some of your pupils will ignore (or pretend to ignore) the flag as it is raised and continue to debate the ins and outs of last night's TV or the latest computer game – so you could always have a few less subtle options available to attract the hardliners. Why not have the national anthem of your chosen country ready to play on CD or MP3 (you could even teach your pupils the words and get them to sing along whenever they hear it)? A hat or piece of national costume is another idea; whenever you don that item of clothing, all chat in English must stop as your class is whisked to the new land.

If you want to really impress the other classes in your school (and become the talk of the staffroom) add a second or even a third flag to your arsenal, forcing your pupils to switch from one set of foreign language phrases to another as the location is changed. Wunderbar!

If you want to use this exercise with younger pupils who may not be able to learn as many foreign phrases as their older schoolmates, why not learn a song or nursery rhyme that originates from your chosen country?

So, if you were to display a French flag, the class would be required to stop talking and sing 'Frère Jacques':

Frère Jacques, Frère Jacques
Dormez vous? Dormez vous
Sonnez les matines, Sonnez les matines
Din, din, don! Din, din, don!

Should the flag of Scotland be raised, your pupils must recite the nursery rhyme, 'Aiken Drum':

There was a man lived in the moon
Lived in the moon, lived in the moon
There was a man lived in the moon
And his name was Aiken Drum

CHORUS

And he played upon a ladle, a ladle, a ladle
And he played upon a ladle, and his name was Aiken Drum

And his hat was made of good cream cheese
Of good cream cheese, of good cream cheese
And his hat was made of good cream cheese
And his name was Aiken Drum.

CHORUS

And his coat was made of good roast beef
Of good roast beef, of good roast beef
And his coat was made of good roast beef
And his name was Aiken Drum

CHORUS

And his buttons made of penny loaves
Of penny loaves, of penny loaves
And his buttons made of penny loaves
And his name was Aiken Drum

CHORUS

And his breeches made of haggis bags
Of haggis bags, of haggis bags
And his breeches made of haggis bags
And his name was Aiken Drum

Reverse

Sometimes, the best way to stop pupils talking is to give them something even more fun to do – and what's more fun than doing everything backwards?

Upon your command (which can be anything from just shouting the word 'Reverse!' to putting on your jacket back to front) your pupils must switch into reverse gear and immediately work backwards through what they have been doing. So, if they've been getting out their workbooks and pencils, they must put them away; if they were reading a story, they have to turn back a page and read from the bottom to the top; and if they've been eating their fruit . . . well, if you play the game as they're doing that, you deserve everything you get!

It is important to stress to your pupils that they should not try to walk around the room in reverse. Negotiating obstacles such as tables, chairs and other classmates when you can't see where you are going is not to be encouraged. Everything should be done from a sitting position.

Best of all, your pupils must talk in reverse while all this is happening. Now, you *could* just get them to make up a random string of nonsense words that sounds as if they're speaking backwards, or you could get everyone to write down some commonly used words and try to work out how they would sound if they were spelled the other way round. For example:

WORD	REVERSED	PRONUNCIATION
class	ssalc	salk
school	loohcs	looks
my	ym	yime
teacher	rehcaet	raykate
pupil	lipup	lipup
pencil	licnep	licknep
backwards	sdrawkcab	strawkab
drama	amard	amard

As you can see, some of the letter combinations don't work very well when written backwards. If this happens, encourage your pupils to reverse the *sound* of the syllable, rather than struggle with an odd sequence of letters. In this way, a simple sentence like 'where is my pencil?' would be pronounced in reverse: 'licknep see yime earew?'

Try asking everyone to work out what their name would sound like if it was spoken backwards, breaking it down if it becomes too difficult to say. My name – Tommy Donbavand – becomes Da Navab Nod Yamot. These are the names your pupils should be called for the duration of this activity, so it might be worth asking everyone to make a sticker with their new moniker and practising yourself!

If you really want to have some fun with this exercise, open the Sound Recorder program on any Windows computer and record a few short phrases. Now, simply click on 'Reverse' in the 'Effects' menu, and your class will hear what they sound like speaking backwards!

Once everyone has worked out how to write and say their name in reverse, you have a great opportunity for an activity that looks at the personalities of your pupils and their friends.

Get everyone to write and illustrate a story about their backwards persona. Remind your pupils that these new characters will have the opposite interests and skills to themselves – and they'll look different, too. So, if one of your male pupils is particularly tall, his reverse character will be short. If a girl in the group is adept at singing, her alter ego will be tone deaf. Got someone in the class who's hot-tempered? That's one chilled-out dude in this world!

Not only will this be a fun creative writing project, but it will inspire your class to look closer than usual at their strengths and abilities.

Silence is golden

Do you use Golden Time as a way to reward your pupils for good behaviour at the end of the day or week? If you do, here's a quick and easy way to use this treat to achieve instant silence.

All you need is a golden-coloured prop to keep on your desk, from a simple shape cut from gold card to something as impressive as a gold statuette (if, by some chance, you haven't received the Oscar for Best Supporting Actor in a motion picture, you'll find trophies made from gold-painted plastic in most sports shops).

Explain to your pupils that, whenever you hold the golden prop above your head, they must stop talking immediately and that you will subtract one minute from Golden Time for each person who speaks without permission once the item has been raised. So, if five pupils continue to chatter after you've lifted up the precious prop, that's five minutes of fun the class will lose.

You may want to give the class a few seconds' leeway while the whispered word spreads that the golden item is aloft. Then again, you may be one of those modern-thinking, 'soft' teachers who doesn't believe in the use of reinforced steel cages and cattle prods . . .

Up to eleven

The inspiration for this activity comes from the movie *This Is Spinal Tap*, where spoof rock guitarist, Nigel Tufnel, has amplifiers made with dials that go up to 11 because, in his words, 'it's one louder' than amps that only go to 10.

You'll need to make a dial of your own in order to control your classroom volume with this exercise – but it doesn't have to be anything complicated: a cardboard arrow pinned to the centre of a circle of paper will do. If you want to go a step further, glue the top of an aerosol can to the centre of the arrow so that you have something with which to turn it. Finally, write the numbers from 1 to 11 around the outside of the dial, making sure you can turn your arrow to any digit you choose.

Set an acceptable volume level for class when you introduce your dial (7 or 8 would be good numbers to choose) and leave the dial there. Now, when the chatter begins to build, simply move the arrow to a more suitable figure. After a second or two, your pupils will realize that you are adjusting the dial and lower their voices correspondingly.

Strangely, you will find that you always get your pupils to be quieter by instructing them to talk louder first! All you do is turn the dial up, thereby increasing the volume in the classroom (the boys in particular love this part). Then, when you have everyone's attention, you can slowly turn the dial back down to a more acceptable level.

Try not to let the fact that you have power over your pupils' voices go to your head. You'll find that the laughter is *very* noisy if the dial breaks off in your hand!

Sleep!

Are there times when you wish you had a magic wand with which you could cast a sleep spell over the rowdier members of your class? I bet there are – and here's a way to enjoy the next best thing.

Explain to your pupils that, if you walk up behind them, gently squeeze their shoulder and whisper a magic word, then they have had a two-minute long sleep spell cast over them, and they must play along.

When a pupil has been hit by the spell, they have to sit in their seat (if they're not already doing so), stop talking and rest their head in their arms on the desk as though asleep for two minutes. You may get one or two dissenting voices but, once you have explained that two minutes is only 120 seconds (they can even count them off in their heads if they want), they should agree to take part.

Two minutes seems to be a magic time period in which even the chattiest pupil will forget what they were discussing and start thinking about something else – hopefully, the subject at hand!

Now, you *can* just use a familiar magic word such as 'abracadabra' for your magic spell – but you could use your preparation for this activity as a launch pad to discuss the power of words and language.

The spells your pupils are likely to be familiar with include those used in the Harry Potter books by J. K. Rowling, such as:

Lumos – creates a light at the end of your wand
Wingardium Leviosa – makes objects fly
Riddikulus – makes scary objects seem funny
Petrificus Totalus – freezes a person rigid
Sonorus – amplifies your voice

Talk about the words used to create those spells, then discuss ideas for creating a sleep spell of your very own. Sleepers often dream, so *Dreamia!* could be used or, for a funnier spell, you could try *Snorus!*

If you want to take this exercise even further, why not invent two or three different magic spells? Perhaps you could use one that 'levitates' your pupils to their places on the carpet when used (they have to act as though they're flying), or a spell that freezes everyone in their current position until you order their release?

Buy or make a magic wand and, with the power of these spells at your fingertips, you'll find that your pupils actually enjoy being told what to do. Magic!

Mime machine

It's time to mime in this fast and fun activity that requires no preparation, other than to explain the rules.

Whenever your pupils become a little rowdy, shout out the word 'Mime!' and they must each carry on exactly what they're doing – talking, reading, writing, etc. – except it must now all be performed in silent mime. After a few seconds, everyone will be concentrating so hard on getting their mimes right, that their conversations will be long forgotten.

If you want to make more of your mimes, why not spend some time practising the art of acting without voice or props. It's tougher than it looks and, although everyone's first instinct is to pretend they're trapped inside a glass box, miming even basic tasks can take a while to get right. Try these out for size, first with the props concerned, and then without:

- *Reading a book* – make sure your mimed pages aren't changing in size. Try to keep your hand at a uniform distance from where the spine would be when you turn over.
- *Making a cup of tea* – you'll be surprised how much your cup moves around between pouring in the water, adding the milk and spooning the sugar. Don't forget to hold your cup by its handle, or you'll drop it!
- *Painting a portrait* – remember where your canvas is, and make sure the tip of your brush touches it with each stroke. It's easy to put your hand through the painting.

When your class has had a little practice, try miming a group event, such as a rock concert or a game of football. Everyone will need to concentrate hard to create the illusion required.

Sound effect story

As I mentioned earlier in this chapter – sometimes, the best way to keep your pupils quiet is to let them be noisy for a while first. This exercise is a way of getting the desire to be loud out of everyone's system in one go.

Although I've chosen a traditional story to explain the activity (albeit with a twist at the end), you can use any story you want – ideal if you're working on a tale with the class and you want to explore it further. Be warned, however, this exercise gets very noisy – so you may want to warn other teachers of your plan!

What follows is the script for the entire story, with what your pupils should be doing shown in parentheses (like this).

If you really want to go to town, you can merge this exercise with the previous miming activity and have your pupils act out the story on the spot as they make the noises with their voices.

Here's the script . . .

Little Red Riding Hood

As I tell you this story, I want you to help me by creating the sound effects for the story using just your voices. Do you think you can do that? (Yes!) I said, do you think you can do that? (YES!)

OK, let's have a practice . . . Imagine that I said that there was a dog in the story – what would that sound like? (Woof, woof!) Now, come on; I know you can be louder than that. What does the dog sound like? (WOOF, WOOF!) Very good! Now, what if it was a tiny little dog . . . What would that sound like? (Woof, woof/Yip, yip!) Great! OK – what if it was a big dog – but far, far away? (Woof, woof!) No, it's much further away than that, so it would be quieter . . . (Woof, woof!)

Fantastic! Now – let's get on with the story . . .

Once upon a time, there was a girl called Little Red Riding Hood and, one day, she went walking through the forest with a basket of cakes and sandwiches that she was taking to Grandma's house for tea. The wind was blowing through the trees   . (one or two pupils wil remember to make noises!) I said, the wind was blowing through the trees! (Whooooo!) The birds were tweeting, high in the branches . . . (Tweet, tweet!) The twigs were snapping under Little Red Riding Hood's feet . . . (Snap, snap!) Well, twigs don't actually say 'Snap!' when you step on them, do they? They make a kind of cracking noise . . . (Crick, crick!) And, as she was walking, Little Red Riding Hood was singing a little song to herself . . . (La, la lah!)

Suddenly, Little Red Riding Hood heard the roar of the Big Bad Wolf – who was very far away indeed . . . (ROAR!) No, he was much further away than that . . . (Roar!) That's better. Little Red Riding Hood was a tiny bit scared, so she gave out a tiny scream! (Argh!)

But, she carried on walking to Grandma's house. The wind was blowing through the trees . . . (a half-hearted 'Whoo!'!) I said, the wind was blowing through the trees! (Whooooo!) The birds were tweeting, high in the branches . . . (Tweet, tweet!) The twigs were snapping under Little Red Riding Hood's feet . . . (Crick, crick!) And, as she was walking, Little Red Riding Hood was singing a little song to herself . . . (La, la lah!)

Just then, Little Red Riding Hood heard the roar of the Big Bad Wolf again and, this time, he was a little bit closer . . . (Roar!) And Little Red Riding Hood was a little more scared, so she gave out a slightly bigger scream! (Argh!)

[For optimum effect, begin to talk faster here] But, she carried on walking to Grandma's house. The wind was blowing through the trees . . . (Whooooo!) The birds were tweeting, high in the branches . . . (Tweet, tweet!) The twigs were snapping under Little Red Riding Hood's feet . . . (Crick, crick!) And, as she was walking, Little Red Riding Hood was singing a little song to herself . . . (La, la lah!)

Just then, Little Red Riding Hood heard the roar of the Big Bad Wolf again and, this time, he was very close indeed . . . (Roar!) And Little Red Riding Hood was very scared, so she gave out a bigger scream! (Argh!)

[Talk faster still] But, she carried on walking to Grandma's house. The wind was blowing through the trees . . . (Whooooo!) The birds were tweeting, high in the branches . . . (Tweet, tweet!) The twigs were snapping under Little Red Riding Hood's feet . . . (Crick, crick!) And, as she was walking, Little Red Riding Hood was singing a little song to herself . . . (La, la lah!)

Suddenly – the Big Bad Wolf jumped out in front of Little Red Riding Hood, and he roared at the top of his voice! (ROAR!) And that made Little Red Riding Hood scream at the top of her voice! (ARGH!) And that made the wolf roar even louder! (ROAR!) And that made Little Red Riding Hood scream even louder! (ARGH!) And that made the wolf roar even louder! (ROAR!) And that made Little Red Riding Hood scream even louder! (ARGH!)

Suddenly, there was silence! Little Red Riding Hood looked at the Big Bad Wolf and said, 'Oh my! What big eyes you've got!'

The wolf replied, 'All the better to see you with!'

'Oh my!' said Little Red Riding Hood. 'What big ears you've got!'

'All the better to hear you with!' replied the wolf.

'Oh my!' said Little Red Riding Hood. 'What big teeth you've got!'

'All the better to eat you with,' roared the wolf – and he was just about to pounce on Little Red Riding Hood when she reached into her basket of cakes and sandwiches and pulled out a light sabre! What noise does a light sabre make? (Zhumm, zhumm!)

This time it was the wolf's turn to scream as Little Red Riding Hood chopped him into a hundred pieces and, when she was finished, she picked up all the pieces of wolf and hid them inside the cakes and sandwiches. So, Grandma had wolf for tea and never even knew about it! (Urgh!)

The end!

Everyone will be too exhausted to chat after that!

If you're working with younger pupils, make sure you have a couple of classroom assistants nearby as one or two of the children may find the roaring and screaming a little scary. And, of course – where early years are concerned – the Big Bad Wolf simply runs away at the sight of Little Red Riding Hood's light sabre, and is never seen again!

Zoo knew?

A very quick and easy exercise that makes use of your pupils' need to concentrate on the task at hand to wipe any thought of chatter from their minds.

At your signal (perhaps you reveal a picture of a zoo entrance, or don a zoo keeper's hat) your class must continue with their conversations but, instead of speaking any human language, they must instantly switch to animal sounds.

It's up to your pupils which animal they choose to become (although a lot of the boys will choose monkeys!), so you could award points for the most original choice of creature.

Of course, if there is a particular species or part of the world you are studying, this activity can easily be tied in with those lessons. If, for example, you're looking at the African savannah – your pupils could be instructed to mimic the animals found there (lions, zebras and even meerkats). If the rainforest is your topic, your classroom could soon be filled with the sounds of orang-utans, toucans and red-eyed tree frogs!

Obviously, it is difficult to accurately describe the sounds made by these creatures in the pages of a book but, if you fire up a computer and pay a visit to websites such as:

www.partnersinrhyme.com/soundfx/animals/Safari.shtml

and

www.educypedia.be/education/animalmoviessounds.htm

. . . you'll be able to download and play real-life animal sounds for your pupils to impersonate. Once they have mastered the sounds, the rest is up to their imaginations. Just how would a zebra describe the goals in last night's football match? Can a macaw really arrange a weekend shopping trip with its friends? You'll find that everyone will be so busy getting their animal calls right, they'll quickly forget the topics of conversation that, until a few moments ago, they found so fascinating.

(Remember that the internet is always changing. Websites come and go very quickly so, if the sites listed above don't appear to be available, simply head to your favourite search engine and see what you can find by entering 'animal sounds'.)

Do you copy?

A fast and furious repeat-after-me game that will get everyone in the class saying exactly what you want them to say!

As with many of these exercises, you'll need a signal that the game is in play to use whenever the talking gets a little too loud. In this case, it would be simple to simply shout the phrase 'Do you copy?' but, as ever, if you can find a way to adapt the activity to better suit your class – go right ahead.

At the signal that the game has begun, everyone must repeat what you say – exactly how you say it. It may take you a few phrases to get everyone on board but, before long, your pupils will be listening hard instead of speaking.

Try to use sentences that start with 'I' because, when repeated back to you, your pupils will find themselves promising to be quiet, concentrate on their work and much more. You'll be surprised how effective a group call and response can be to drumming an idea into the collective mind.

Try these phrases out:

- 'I will lower my voice!'
- 'I do not need to be talking to complete this task!'
- 'I will concentrate on what I am doing!'
- 'I will stop chatting and start working!'

When you have everybody's attention, try dropping in one or two of these suggestions – just for fun:

- 'I want to have worms on toast for lunch today!'
- 'I would like extra homework this week!'
- 'My teacher is a superstar!'

You'll find that, once you've got everyone giggling at these funny phrases, the class will be content to settle down and work quietly.

To end the game – have another command that everyone knows is the signal to stop copying what you say. Something like 'Stop copying now!' would work.

Copy that?

Slowmo

The final exercise in the 'Chatterboxes' chapter lets you take things nice and slow – in fact, right down to slow motion!

A handy prop to acquire for this game would be an old TV remote control unit (the bigger the better) but, if you can't locate one, why not make a huge imitation from an empty cereal box? You'll need four buttons on your oversized remote: SLOW, SLOWER, SLOWEST and STOP. These could be made by gluing matchboxes onto the cereal packet, or simply by painting different coloured squares. Once you have your remote, fix it to the wall where everyone can see it.

When the class starts to get a little too rowdy, reach up and press your finger on the SLOW button. After a few seconds, word will spread round the classroom that you are activating the remote (there's *always* at least one pupil who keeps a sharp eye on the teacher at all times!).

As soon as your pupils see that you are pressing the SLOW button, they must continue exactly what they are doing (including talking), only now everything must be done at half speed.

When you're satisfied that everyone has dropped down a gear, move your finger over to the SLOWER button. Once again, the entire class has to continue with the activity and conversation at hand, but must now move and speak at an even slower pace. It's not as easy as it sounds – especially when everyone tends to go far too slowly on the first command!

Things get really tough when you switch to the SLOWEST button. Now your pupils should be moving and speaking at a snail's pace (you may even see a vast improvement in some of your pupils' handwriting now they're taking their time!).

When you're finally ready for some peace and quiet, press the STOP button. This acts as a kind of 'freeze' command where your pupils have to stop what they're doing and saying and listen to you. Now's the time to explain that you need a little more hush while everyone is working (no one is allowed to react or respond, remember – so they'll have to pay attention!).

When you've got your message across (or you feel your class has been perfectly still for long enough), work your way back up through the buttons – starting with SLOWEST, then SLOWER, SLOW and, eventually, taking your finger away from the controls. Everyone should now get on with their work in a much calmer, more relaxed atmosphere.

Of course, if you want to have a little fun with your class, there's nothing to stop you adding an extra row of buttons: FAST, FASTER, FASTEST and BLUR! make sure to instruct the class to stay in their seats, however. There's nothing more likely to cause an accident than a boisterous boy trying to show you how quickly he can move around the room!

2 Attention!

As children become surrounded more and more by computer games, DVDs and the internet, so their ability to concentrate is eroded. Indeed, some studies are now suggesting that the average attention span of a child equates to one minute for each year of their lives. So, if you're teaching a class of seven and eight year olds, you may well have lost them all within ten minutes. It's a sobering thought.

Fortunately, concentration can be trained and attention strengthened. What follows is a series of games, exercises and activities that either help your pupils to focus for longer periods of time, or can be used to grab their attentions when minds begin to wander.

As with all the activities in this book – feel free to adapt and alter the exercises to best suit your teaching style and current lessons. This chapter is unique, however, in that you will be asked to make a bit of a fool of yourself in order to grab focus and keep it. Trust me, there is nothing that turns all eyes on the room towards you than not knowing what you'll do next!

Now, on with the ideas before your mind begins to wander . . .

Instant boots

This game was originally created to pass time on long journeys, but I soon found it could be used to capture the attention of the children I was working with. Try it out and see if it works for your class.

The premise is simple; two words (an adjective and a noun) are chosen at random and paired together. Whatever this new phrase suggests, the person running the game (in this case – you) must act out without hesitation, portraying the first thing that comes to mind.

So, taking the game's title – if you were given the phrase 'instant boots', you might begin to march on the spot, pretend to hike up a steep hill, or even mime taking a shot at goal in a football match. It is up to the rest of the group (your pupils) to work out how you have interpreted the command.

What springs to mind when you are presented with the following pairs of words? (my suggestions are in parentheses):

- Unhappy aeroplane (arms out, crying, looking for a place to land)
- Sudden computer (surprise as a PC appears, then you settle down to type)
- Terrifying crabs (horror as your hands become crabs crawling up your body)
- Fast pencil (picking up a pencil to write, then being dragged along as it does so)
- Important music (mime putting a CD in, pressing play, then leaping to attention)
- Missing telephone (make to pick up the telephone receiver, then realize it's gone).

Can you stand up and act out a short, improvised mime of your own suggested by each of those phrases? As I mentioned in the introduction to this chapter – you are going to have to make a bit of a fool of yourself. Sorry!

To use the game in a classroom situation, make two stacks of cards: one pile with an adjective written on each, and the other with a noun on each. Now, when you want the class's attention, announce the start of the game by shouting 'Instant boots!' and nominating two of your pupils to collect a card – one from each pile.

Whatever phrase is made up by the two cards, you must act out – no matter how silly the suggestion or how ridiculous you feel. Trust me – you'll lose their attention very quickly if you refuse to perform once you've promised them a show!

No matter what you do, you'll find that the moment is enough to wipe whatever they were thinking from their minds, and encourage them all to listen to you.

If you're working with older pupils, you may find that the adjective and noun combination can be a little too limiting for their more sophisticated sense of humour. If this is the case, try pairing an adjective with a verb to see what happens.

Be warned, however, the results are occasionally difficult to act out and can be very, very surreal! How would you perform these phrases (again with my ideas):

- Distant thinking (looking thoughtful on one side of the room, then the other)
- Famous running (jogging while signing autographs and shaking hands)
- Eventual driving (sitting in a car then, after a moment, grabbing the wheel)
- Wooden writing (chop down a tree, then use it to write a letter).

Once you've acted out one of those, your pupils will all be watching you carefully – if for no other reason than to see if your mind is about to snap!

Next!

This is my version of a traditional drama exercise used in acting classes around the world. It will take anything up to half an hour to complete but, if you run the game on a fairly regular basis, you'll discover that your pupils' ability to concentrate is on the increase.

Gather the class together in a circle, with you standing in the centre. It might be a good idea to use the school hall, if you have access to it, or simply push the desks back to create a space in your own room.

To play the game, choose two pupils to come into the centre of the circle, and explain that you are going to give them a short piece of drama to act out. I always start with a scene where a customer comes into a shop wanting to buy a box of cornflakes, but the assistant is new and doesn't know where they are kept.

You may find that your pupils are a little shy and, especially if they are older, will giggle their way through this first scene. Stick with the game, as they'll settle into it once they realize how much fun it can be.

Once the scene is progressing, wait for a suitable moment to clap your hands and shout 'Freeze!' (in the set-up with the shop, I always wait until the customer points to wherever the cornflakes are stored). Both players must immediately stop exactly where they are, in whatever position they find themselves.

Choose one of the players to go back to their place in the circle, leaving one of your pupils frozen in their pose in the centre (I usually choose whoever is playing the customer character, still pointing off to their beloved cornflakes).

Now it is time for another pupil to enter the circle and start a new scene with the frozen actor. The new scene must begin with the current pose (in this case, the pointing finger) but must change whatever is happening into something new. So, in this case, the outstretched finger could be pressing a button, poking a rival in the chest or even picking another person's nose!

Of course, the pupil currently frozen in position will not know what the new scene will entail, and so it is up to the new player to start the scene by saying a line that will tell both their fellow actor and the rest of the group what is happening. The other person involved in the drama must pick up on the new direction and act along.

So, the new player may come in and shout, 'Don't press that button! That sets off the missiles!' The first player could then take on the guise of a bad guy and boast about how he will rule the world once he has shown everyone what he can do!

From exactly the same pose, the new player could position their chest against the extended finger of their friend and pretend they have just been poked. 'Don't poke me – I'm just trying to point out that you've made a mistake! Fish cannot fly!'

The final example involves the new actor sliding one of their nostrils over the end of the finger, and you don't need me to either describe that scene to you, or to tell you which of your pupils would be the most likely to choose that scenario (admit it – you're picturing that very child right now!).

What the new player must NOT do is start the new scene by saying anything ambiguous. Sentences like, 'What are you doing?' or 'What are you pointing at?' do not tell the frozen actor or the rest of the group what the new scene is about; it puts responsibility onto the other pupil, and that's not what this exercise is for.

When the new scene has started, allow the two actors to follow it through for a moment or two until another interesting pose comes about, then clap and shout 'Freeze!' once more, ask one of the pupils to sit down and begin again from this new frozen position.

You'll find that, the first time you run this exercise, a lot of your pupils will sit in silence around the edges of the circle while the same contenders raise their hands with idea after idea. Whether you want everyone to take a turn is up to you but, in my experience, the shyer members of the group won't perform well if they are forced to take part.

It could be that they simply don't have any suggestions for what the new scenes could be about (some pupils have less of an imagination than others), so one way to involve them is to ask those players who are constantly raising their hands to whisper their ideas to a friend who hasn't yet had a turn. You may find that, once they have a potential plot in mind, they enjoy the actual acting part.

Some pupils simply won't get involved. However, the more you run this exercise, the more they'll get used to the idea that it's OK to stand up in front of their friends and pretend to be someone or something else (after all, that's what they've spent dozens of playtimes doing since they first started school!). Even just watching their classmates taking part is enough to start expanding their level of concentration.

Before long, your pupils will be calling, 'Me! Me!' and begging to be the person to start the new scene, and all you'll have to do is choose one of the many raised hands, saying 'Next!'

Tell a lie

Not that I'm one to promote the speaking of untruths but, the fact remains that if you insert the occasional obvious lie into your classes, your pupils will sit up and pay attention. What's more – the bigger the whopper, the quicker they'll do so.

The next time you're in the midst of teaching a topic that fails to grip the imaginations of your pupils (for me, it was always arable farming . . .), try slipping in that you're actually an alien life form, and you're on Earth in disguise to help prepare plans for a full-scale invasion. Trust me – everyone will be listening.

Now that the lie is out in the open, inform your class that they have ten questions they can ask about what you've just said (in this case, they can ask about the impending enslavement of the human race). Answering the queries will exercise your imagination just as much as it will your pupils' and, once the allotted number of questions have been asked, resume your previously scheduled lesson. All ears will be trained in your direction in case you let another secret slip and, as a result, the odd fact or two might just creep in and stick there.

Try using these funny fibs whenever you want to shock the class into paying attention:

- 'I once built an undersea village and became mayor to the local fish.'
- 'I am really a robot from the future.'
- 'I used to be the Queen's official nose-picker.'
- 'My insides are made of solid gold and diamonds.'
- 'I am actually a zombie, risen from the grave to consume your brains.'
- 'When you go out to play, I stay inside and drink blood.'

Just be sure not to use this activity too frequently, or the novelty will wear off and you may find yourself inventing bigger and more outlandish lies in order to arouse your pupil's interest.

You can use this activity as a way to kick start a creative writing session. After all, what is fiction other than well-crafted lying?

Ask your pupils to think up an untruth about themselves, similar to those you've been using in class. Now, explain that they have to write a 1,000-word story in the first person (i.e. told from the character's point of view: 'I did this', 'I said that', etc.) that expands upon the lie and treats the fib as fact.

You'll find that the class are more than happy to lie about themselves and their accomplishments, and they'll quickly exaggerate the falsehood into a story with a beginning, middle and an end. And that's no word of a lie . . .

Who am I?

Another exercise to get your pupils thinking and, as a result, help expand their attention span into something less fleeting than a bolt of lightning!

All you have to do is think of a famous person – either a celebrity, sports star or even a well-known fictional character. Now your pupils simply have to question you as if you were that person in order to ascertain your new identity. The catch? they can only ask questions that can be answered with a 'Yes!' or 'No!' answer.

So, let's say you had chosen to be Mickey Mouse for the duration of the game (don't worry – you don't have speak in a high-pitched voice or deal with hordes of magical, bucket-carrying broomsticks!). Just be ready to answer your class's questions from Mickey's point of view.

This could be the potential line of questioning: 'Are you male?' (Yes!) Then, 'Are you a footballer?' (No!) 'Are you alive?' (often asked in case you are a famous figure who has passed away, such as Charlie Chaplin or Winston Churchill. In this case, even though Mickey Mouse is fictional, your answer would be 'Yes!')

The interrogation should continue until one of your pupils has narrowed the choices down enough in their mind to hazard a guess as to who you might be. (Male, not a footballer, alive, not human, a cartoon character, not a duck, etc.) There is no penalty for making an incorrect guess as to your hidden identity, but the pupil concerned will have to wait their turn to try and guess again.

Make sure to explain that you can only answer questions with a 'Yes!' or a 'No!' You'll be amazed how many times you are asked, 'Are you a man or a woman?' or 'Where do you live?' – especially at first.

Occasionally, you'll come across a question to which you genuinely don't know the answer (did David Beckham ever have a trial for Everton football club, for example). In this case, you must simply say that you don't know, and advise your pupils not to consider that fact when deducing who the personality might be.

You'll find that, the more you play this game, the smarter and more on topic the questions will become and that your pupils will arrive at your chosen identity a lot faster than they used to. Evidence of a growing level of concentration if ever you needed it – or my name's not Oliver Hardy!

The very same activity can be used when creating characters for a short story. All your pupils have to do is imagine their character as a 'blank' person, with no history or background, then ask the same sort of questions they would when playing the game – only this time, they are allowed to ask questions that do not require a 'Yes!' or 'No!' response.

They should then choose the most interesting replies to their questions and write them down. ('Where did you go to school?' 'I couldn't go to normal school because I'm allergic to pencils, so I was educated at home by my Gran!')

Before long your pupils will each have a strong, three-dimensional character with a varied and interesting background to use in their tale.

It's a draw!

It's sadly a familiar feeling that, when you're busy adding your intricately prepared lesson to the board, interest in the topic at hand is fading and attentions are already far beyond the four walls of your classroom. What can you do to drag everyone back to where they should be in such a case? Just draw!

This activity has the benefit of being able to grab your class's attention, turning their focus back to the part of the room you want it (the board), and it helps to exercise the group's imagination, too!

Break off from what you're doing and begin to draw a picture on the board. It doesn't matter how good the artwork is, what is important is that your pupils will – one by one – snap out of their daydreams in order to work out what it is. All eyes will be pointed in your direction if there are points or prizes on offer!

Start things simple and sketch a simple picture that's relatively easy to identify and choose from one of the many raised hands around the room willing to take a guess at what your drawing might be.

To make things more interesting, try drawing a phrase or saying in picture form. An eyeball followed by a tin of beans, a picture of an ocean wave and a sheep with long eyelashes could mean: Eye can sea ewe (I can see you).

If you can make your sketches fit in with the topic you're currently teaching, all the better. You'll soon have everyone's undivided attention, and maybe even the job of illustrating the next edition of the school newsletter!

All shopped out!

Your pupils don't need to be shopaholics to take part in this game designed to improve memory and increase concentration levels – they just need to have fun! It's a very simple exercise and, chances are, you've played a version of this game yourself at some point.

Ideally, sit your pupils in a circle – although the game can be played just as effectively in normal classroom seating. The idea of the game is to memorize a list of items that could be bought on a shopping trip, and adding to the list as the game progresses.

So, the first player might say, 'I went shopping, and I bought some peanuts.' The next player would have to add to the list with an item of their choice: 'I went shopping, and I bought some peanuts and a DVD player.' The third player could add: 'I went shopping and I bought some peanuts, a DVD player and a bike.'

See if you can keep the list going right around the classroom, with pupils allowed to mime items to help any of their friends who might get stuck. After you've played this a few times, you'll start to see a real improvement in the length of time the list will go without anyone making a mistake. Better memories all round!

If you're playing this game with older pupils, you may need to give them more of a challenge. Try a shopping list in alphabetical order (apples, bananas, cake, etc.) Or even insist that the players can only name items that can be recycled.

For younger children, help them to remember the items on the list by starting each object with the same letter as their first name (Lorna bought lemons, Stuart picked up socks and Claire chose cucumber, etc.) If anyone gets stuck, just remind them to think of the person who first named the item.

Gone!

A quick-fire game that will test everyone's powers of observation . . .

Place a number of everyday school items on a table, such as a pencil, a ruler, a paper clip, etc. Around 20 items will make the game an enjoyable challenge. Allow everyone 30 seconds to examine the items on the table, then cover everything with a sheet or large cloth.

Remove one of the items without your pupils seeing (you may have to ask them to close their eyes), then pull the cloth away. Your pupils have ten seconds to identify which object is missing.

There are several variations of this game to try when your class becomes adept at spotting which of the items you have taken away. Try moving the remaining objects around to make it harder to spot what has gone. Or, add a new item to the group and have your pupils guess which of the objects has just arrived.

To make things really tough – don't add or take anything away, just turn one of the items beneath the sheet into a new position or angle. Your pupils will really have to concentrate to tell which object has been moved.

Mind's eye

Just how much information are your pupils taking in about the world around them? How often have you changed a display in the classroom only to have no one notice it at all? It's time to open up their minds (not literally, of course!).

Ask one of your pupils to approach the board and stand facing it, without looking round. Now, keeping out of their line of vision, ask that pupil to describe what you're wearing today.

Chances are they'll get it completely wrong (much to the amusement of the rest of the class) – but that's to be expected. We can only take in a certain amount of information at a time and something as seemingly unimportant as what someone is wearing doesn't top the list of facts to commit to memory. Yet, what if your pupils were witnesses to an accident or a crime? They might be expected to describe a suspect, or explain what happened over a certain course of events.

Introducing your pupils to the idea that everything around them has the potential to be vital is a great way to help them look at the world – and the lessons you teach – anew. The good news is, it's a relatively simple task to complete.

In advance of the exercise, go around the school and take note of everyday items; maybe the colour of the door to the next classroom along, the title of the largest book on display in the library section, or even the number of tables in the dining room. Now, take your pupils on a walk through the school, telling them that you want them to pay extra attention to what they see.

When you're back in class, hold a short quiz asking for information about what you saw on your walk. Chances are they won't have picked up on any of the things you ask them about and the scores will be uniformly low. Time to go for another walk . . .

This time, your pupils will know to look at their surroundings differently. Explain that you'll be asking a different set of questions this time (so they don't all stand and count the dining room tables), but don't give away anything else. When you run the quiz at the end of this trip, you'll see an improvement in the results.

After a few such expeditions, you'll be amazed at what your class begins to see – and they'll even start asking you questions that you can't answer without a second look!

If you really want to test their new-found powers of observation, take your class on a walk outside and make notes as you go about your surroundings (maybe the colours of the cars parked in a particular place, or the items on sale in a certain shop window). Your pupils will be taking everything in, just in case you include it in your end of walk quiz!

You can capitalize on this new 'open eyes' way of thinking by changing something around the room (such as the position of two pictures) before the pupils arrive and offering points to anyone who can tell what is different.

They'll never look at things the same way again.

Younger pupils simply can't take in the same amount of information as their older classmates, and so you will have to ask them questions on something with which they are a little more familiar – such as a favourite TV show or movie.

If you have the facilities, show an episode of an age-appropriate TV show, or a section from a movie – then ask questions about what they watched. What colour T-shirt was the main character wearing? How many times did the bad guy fall down? What was the name of the person with the blue hat?

Rather than just providing the answers, you'll find it more satisfying to re-watch the episode and have your pupils point out the answers as they go. They'll all be watching a lot closer this time!

Do the clue

Another observation-based activity that will have everyone paying attention as they watch for subtle – and not so sutble – clues.

Explain to your class that you will be giving out clues to a famous place throughout the course of the day – but do not say what form the clues will take (that way, pupils will have to keep their eyes peeled and ears open at all times!).

In advance, choose a familiar landmark or place, such as the Eiffel Tower (if you can fit the location into your current lesson plans – all the better). Now, prepare a series of clues that you could introduce to your class throughout the day. For the Eiffel Tower, these might include:

- A small French flag
- A piece of iron

- The French national anthem
- A map of Paris
- A figure representing the height of the tower (320 metres).

During the normal course of lessons throughout the day, introduce these clues one at a time, but do not draw particular attention to them. Perhaps you could use a lump of iron as a new paperweight on your desk (the Eiffel Tower is made up of 18,038 pieces of 'puddled' or very pure construction iron), or maybe whistle the national anthem of France as you write something up on the board.

The idea is not for your pupils to guess as each clue is presented, but to add all the clues together ready to submit an answer at the end of the day. A fun way to do this is to have slips of paper on which pupils can write their name and their answer, and a special box in which to post their suggestions. After lessons have finished for the day, collect all the answer slips and award points to everyone who guessed correctly.

When you reveal the result and the winners the following morning, you may find yourself surprised as to what some of your class took to be clues. If this happens, award yourself a pat on the back as it means they were concentrating much harder than usual!

List and tell

This traditional party game is another great way to help your pupils exercise their memories and sharpen their thought processes into the bargain.

To prepare for the activity, you'll need to make a set of cards, on each of which is listed a topic such as 'animals', 'movies', 'books' or 'food'. When the game starts, simply choose one of these cards at random and show it to your class.

Your pupils must now take turns to name items that belong in that topic, but must not repeat something another pupil has said. So, if the chosen topic was animals, each player would need to name an animal in turn (lion, parrot, ant, etc.) The idea is to try and keep going until everyone in the class has had a turn.

If someone repeats an item or object that has already been named – a new topic card is chosen and play starts again. How many tries will it take your class to get all the way round in one go?

If you really want to test your pupils' thinking power make the topics more difficult and relevant to what they've been learning recently. Can everyone name a 'job in nineteenth-century Britain', or one of the 'rivers of the world'?

Shock treatment

A final quick and fun way to get the whole class hanging off your every word. In advance, arrange a certain number of key phrases that you want your pupils to listen out for throughout the day – then assign a certain action or response to each of those phrases.

For example, you might decide that, every time you say 'shark!' to your pupils, they must get their feet out of the water (off the floor) as quickly as they can or they'll lose a limb to a prowling great white. Maybe you could suggest that, whenever you announce the arrival of 'vampire bats!', everyone has to get underneath their tables before the bloodsucking creatures swoop down and start feasting.

Choose around five phrases and practise the moves associated with each one until everyone is clear what they have to do when that commend is given. Now, simply drop those phrases into your lessons throughout the day and watch as the class responds. 'The area of a circle can be determined by use of the – poltergeist attack – formula.'

You'll find that, the first few times you utter one of the chosen phrases, not everyone will react with the same speed or urgency. That's because only some of the class were paying attention. However, everyone will be listening out for the next phrase hidden somewhere in that day's lessons.

You will, of course, have to repeat what you were saying when you uttered the words that caused everyone to react – but you can bet that everyone will be taking it all in by now!

3 Wash your mouth out!

You can say a lot with a few words. Consider the emotion contained in Ernest Hemingway's shortest of short stories:

For sale: baby shoes. Never worn.

In just six words, we know what has happened and can imagine the grief that must have been experienced as a result of this tragedy. A wonderful example of the power of language. So why is it that words are abused so much?

No matter how hard you try, some of your pupils will always use inappropriate language. Whether it's swearing, personal insults or even verbal bullying, the usual course of action is to simply clamp down on the offender and reprimand them.

However, there is a school of thought that says children use bad words because they do not have a secure enough grasp of the language – or a large enough vocabulary – to be able to express their feelings effectively. So, instead of just disciplining pupils who resort to unsuitable language, could helping them to expand their word power cut down on the cussing?

It has been my experience that, when given an alternate outlet for their voices, the use of bad language drops considerably. Here are some of the exercises I have used to cut the toilet talk; try them out with your class.

Can I have a word?

Plenty of people get by perfectly well without the ability to speak the same language as those around them – they use a combination of gestures and emphasis in what they say to get their meaning across. So, how can you explain to your pupils that they don't need to use bad language to express how they're feeling? One way is to limit their vocabulary to a single word.

Ask your pupils to get into pairs and explain that they are going to have a conversation with their partner – but they are only allowed to use a single word each. So, if the words chosen were 'duck' and 'cheese', the exchange, 'Good morning, how are you?' 'I'm fine, thanks!' would become 'Duck duck, duck duck duck?' 'Cheese cheese, cheese!'

Aside from raising some giggles, the purpose of the exercise is twofold. First, it demonstrates, albeit rather severely, how difficult it is to express yourself if you lack the sufficient vocabulary. And, secondly, it requires the use the correct emphasis, tone and body language.

Try asking your pupils to say these different phrases out loud, replacing each of the words with a single, unrelated word, such as 'duck':

- 'I love you!'
- 'Please don't scare me!'
- 'Get out of here!'
- 'I'm really tired!'

Your pupils will discover that it is possible to make themselves understood in their conversation without using 'real' words. This shows that they really don't need to use bad language to express their emotions; if they're angry, worried or scared – any words will do, so long as they're expressed in the right way.

A fun way to expand this exercise for older pupils is to set your classroom up as a 'Big Brother' style house (similar to the TV reality show). Choose up to ten pupils to enter the house while the remaining pupils become the viewers at home.

Each of the ten contestants is issued with a single word (as explained above) which they have to use exclusively throughout the game. Now, let the players introduce themselves to each other and set them a task or two.

After 30 minutes or so, ask the viewing pupils to vote for who they want to evict from the house, based purely on how the contestants have behaved, and not on personal friendships or alliances. You'll discover that certain contestants will have become popular with the viewers, and others are quick to be voted against.

Because none of the players have spoken in complete sentences, this must be down to body language, gestures and emphasis on the only word they are allowed to use. Proof positive that it's not what you say – it's how you say it!

Bottle ale rascal

If your pupils insist on hurling insults at one another, why not get them to use and then invent some that are creative, at least?

Shakespeare's work is filled with unusual and original insults – many of which cannot be easily understood and so, when used, are unlikely to cause the same offence as a modern-day curse.

Try these tirades from the bawdy bard:

- Base Ignoble Wretch!
- Clod Of Wayward Marl!
- Curl'd-Pate Ruffian!
- Dog-Fox Not Proved Worth A Blackberry!
- Fatal Screech-Owl!
- Jackanape With Scarves!
- Liege Of All Loiterers And Malcontents!
- Monsieur Mock-Water!
- Prating Mountebank!
- Rump-Fed Ronyon!
- Snipt-Taffeta Fellow!
- Triton Of The Minnows!

Use any of those in a heated discussion and, if nothing else, the conversation will grind to a halt while at least one of the participants tries to work out whether they've just been insulted or not!

See if your pupils can come up with authentic sounding insults of old, and insist that they are the only names used while on school premises. The use of fouler abuse will drop sharply, or I'm not a white-livered runagate!

Yes/No

Another quick-fire way to get your pupils thinking harder about the words they use is to play the old-fashioned Yes/No game.

Quite simply, you choose a pupil to sit in front of you. You then ask that person a series of questions for 60 seconds, in answer to which they must not use the words 'Yes!' or 'No!' Nor can they shake or nod their heads, refuse to answer or hesitate for a period of longer than five seconds.

The best way to play the game is to ask a couple of questions that do not require a yes or no answer, then follow quickly with one that does.

Here are some queries with which to try and catch them out:

- 'Are you ready to start?' (This one gets them almost every time!)
- 'What is your name?'
- 'How old are you?'
- 'Are you sure?'
- 'Do you go to school?'
- 'Which school?'
- 'Do you like school?'
- 'Do you have any hobbies?'
- 'Do you have any brothers or sisters?'
- 'How many?'
- 'No, you don't!' (Often responded to with 'Yes, I do!')

Once a player has said either 'Yes!' or 'No!', their turn is at an end and it's time to choose another pupil to sit in the hot seat. Award points to the pupils who lasted for the entire minute without uttering either of the forbidden words.

Empathy

If your pupils remain unconvinced by the power of words, it may be time to introduce them to the concept of empathy. Empathy is, quite simply, when you understand the emotions and feelings of another person; a technique employed by writers and actors alike (you experience it every time you feel scared when the main character in a book or movie is in dire straits).

What follows is a short story which you can read out to your pupils, asking them to find a space to stand in and act out what you're describing in mime (no sounds or props allowed). It is written in the second person (i.e. you do this, you do that) to really make your pupils feel as though they are actually there.

Make sure that everyone is acting out what you describe. You may find that one or two of your class giggle nervously as the story progresses, and you'll get a scream from just about everyone at the end of the piece – that's empathy in action!

IMPORTANT – in order for your pupils to experience empathy, the script that follows is a short horror story. I recommend that you DO NOT run this activity with children under the age of 9, or with those who may be easily scared by what happens in the tale.

It's a very hot Sunday afternoon, and you're stuck in your room doing homework. You finish one subject and slam the book closed, deciding to go to the shop on the corner and get yourself a cold drink before you start on the next assignment – you have to write a short story with a twist. The trouble is, you don't know what to write about.

You head downstairs and decide to ask the old lady next door if she wants something from the shop while you're there. You walk up her garden path but, just before you knock on the door – you notice scratch marks on the wood around the handle. Pushing the door gently, it swings open . . .

You call the old lady's name, but there's no answer. Part of you wants to turn and run, but you know you have to find out if everything is OK, so you step inside the house. To the left is the kitchen, and you peek inside. The cooker is on, and it looks as though the old lady has been cooking as ingredients are laid out on the counter. Some of them have fallen to the floor and the room looks untidy, as though there has been some kind of struggle.

Opposite the kitchen is the living room. The radio has been knocked to the floor, and a dining chair has been smashed. You stand the chair up, although you have to lean it against the wall as one of the legs has broken off, and you're about to pick up the radio when you hear a scream!

The scream came from upstairs – it was the old lady! Racing up the stairs you dash into the nearest bedroom to find the old lady backed into a corner and, standing over her, is a vampire! The monster bares its fangs and is about to bite, so you think quickly and grab a lamp from the bedside table.

You smash the lamp down on the vampire's head and grab the old lady's hand, dragging her out of the room. You dash down the stairs together just as the vampire recovers from the blow and chases after you.

You tell the old lady that it will be OK once you're outside and you reach for the front door when she grabs hold of your wrist with more strength than you ever imagined she had. You turn to face her and see that her eyes are glowing white – and she has fangs!

The old lady says that it was all a trap! Once they saw you walking up the garden path, she and the other vampire – her son – decided that your blood would be a nice, refreshing drink on such a hot day.

The old lady's son appears behind her and reaches out for you. You push him as hard as you can and he falls backwards into the living room. He lands on the broken leg of the wooden chair and, as it pierces his heart, he vanishes in a cloud of red dust.

The old lady screams, giving you time to dash into the kitchen and grab a handful of garlic from the ingredients on the counter. You throw the garlic at the old lady and watch in horror as she melts from its sting.

Racing outside, you slam the door behind you and try to catch your breath – then you look up and find yourself back in your bedroom. You realize that everything was part of the short story you were writing and it was so exciting that you seemed to get lost inside the adventure.

Sighing with relief, you head downstairs to go and get that cold drink from the shop – and that's when you notice scratch marks around the handle of your own front door . . .

Your pupils may well scream at the last sentence! Explain that, while it may only be a fictional tale, the fact that everyone felt what the main character was experiencing shows the true power of words.

Using bad language or verbally abusing someone else can hurt just as much as physical violence, and so everyone should think twice before using words as a weapon against someone else.

The name game

Another quick and silly game to get everyone using words in a positive way.

Ask your class to stand in a circle, and to think of a word that both describes them as a person and begins with the same letter as their first name – so, you could have Sensible Susan, Artistic Aaron, Excitable Ellen, etc.

Once everyone has chosen a 'new' name, they must now think of an action to accompany their moniker. Perhaps Sensible Susan could fold her arms and look serious, Artistic Aaron could pretend to paint a picture and jumping up and down; smiling is just right for Excitable Ellen!

The aim of the game is to pass the focus from one player to another within the circle. So, Susan could say, 'Sensible Susan to Excitable Ellen!' folding her arms as she says the first name, and jumping up and down as she says the second. Now it's Ellen's turn: 'Excitable Ellen to Artistic Aaron!', again with the actions.

Keep playing until everyone has had at least two turns, and the focus has been passed back and forth across the circle. Now it's time to drop the names . . .

Try playing the game by using the actions that accompanied the names alone. Aaron would begin by pretending to paint a picture then, if he folded his arms and looked serious, everyone would know that he has passed the focus over to Sensible Susan. Susan could fold her arms, then put her hands to the sides of her face and mime a scream – passing play over to Frightened Freddie!

This game works especially well with younger pupils, or with a group who have just met for the first time and are trying to learn each other's names.

Smelly socks

As we discovered earlier in this chapter, words are powerful tools and should be used with care. They can provoke any range of emotions from pure terror to unstoppable giggling. This game concentrates solely on the giggles!

Choose one of your pupils to play the game and bring them to the front of the class to stand with you. Explain that, no matter what you ask them, they MUST give the same answer every time – smelly socks. However, they must not, under any circumstances, smile or laugh.

Put these posers to your po-faced pupil:

- 'What did you have for breakfast?' (Smelly socks.)
- 'What would you like for Christmas?' (Smelly socks.)
- 'Describe the smell in the staff room . . . ' (Smelly socks.)
- 'What kind of sandwiches should I have for lunch?' (Smelly socks.)

Sooner or later, the laughter from the rest of the class will infect the player at the front and they'll begin to giggle. That's the end of their turn, and it's time to choose another willing victim to answer your questions.

For each pupil who steps up to play give them a different ludicrous answer to use, such as: fish face, wobble bottom, chunky bum and slimy snot.

Laugh-tastic!

Poetic licence

If you're still having a problem controlling what your pupils say to each other, try enforcing this ridiculous rule:

> If you must insult each other all the time,
> Everything that you say must rhyme!

Yes, whenever you catch your pupils speaking in a less than civilized manner to one another, insist that their next sentence must rhyme with the unsavoury language that proceeded it. If you enforce this rule strictly enough, even the most foul-mouthed little monsters will begin to think twice about what they say – simply because they'll be forced to use their brains for doing so.

Of course, this exercise leads well into writing poetry in class – something many pupils and teachers alike dread! It needn't be a chore, however – for every host of golden daffodils, there is always a boy standing on a burning deck.

While I'm not suggesting that you regale your pupils with off-colour limericks, the potential for poetry to expand their appreciation of the spoken word is vast. All you have to do is find a style of poem that appeals to your class.

How about these:

> Peter is a furry worm
> He lives inside a bush
> I hit him with a concrete slab
> Now Peter's furry mush

> My sister said of her new flat
> 'There's not enough room to swing a cat!'
> So I asked my grandma, 'Please
> May I borrow your Siamese?'
> I swung it round with all my might
> And do you know – my sister's right!

Or even an adaptation of a classic nursery rhyme:

> Mary had a little lamb
> It's fleece was black as ink
> That's why she kept it in a pen
> (Clever, don't you think?)

Ask your pupils to write a poem that describes one of their classmates, without using that person's name (you can draw names out of a hat to ensure that everyone has a verse written about them). When they're complete, take it in turns to read out your rhymes and see if you can guess who is the subject.

Of course, not all poems rhyme, but your pupils will find it much easier to stick to simple rhyming verses to begin with. Then you can introduce them to more unusual pieces, such as:

> Sloppy
> Stupid
> Screaming
> Smelly
> Simple

Silly
Shrieking
Septic
Strange
Squealing
SISTER!

If any of your pupils rebel against these rhymes and pretend to be too cool for poetry, simply take one of the songs that is currently riding high in the charts and ask them to write out the lyrics. After all, what is a poem if not merely a song without music? Ask them to write new lyrics for their favourite band, and you'll have a roomful of budding bards within seconds!

Chain tale

Here's a simple activity that not only gets your pupils thinking, but can also be used as a springboard to a creative writing session.

Make a set of cards, each with a single word written on it. Now, invite five pupils to the front of the class, and ask each of them to choose a card without looking at what is written on it. When everyone has chosen, ask them to turn their cards over and reveal their words. Let's say, in this case, the words are: *Boy*, *Green*, *Balloon*, *Run* and *Umbrella*.

The pupils now have to invent a story on the spot, speaking for 30 seconds each, and using their chosen word at some point during their turn. In our example, we could end up with a story about a boy who made a new friend on holiday – a curious friend who always wore the colour green and liked to hug trees.

One day, the boy gave his friend a present of a green balloon. The friend was so excited that he took the balloon and started to run with it. He ran so fast that the wind caught the balloon and carried the boy right up into the clouds, where he sparked off a shower of green rain. The boy sheltered beneath an umbrella as he watched his friend float back down to Earth amid this emerald storm.

Now, that may not be Pulitzer Prize winning material, but it is an original story that those five pupils can take back to their group and expand upon. Maybe they want to write the tale as a children's book, perform it as a piece of drama or even draw posters to show the environmental effects of green rainfall.

Choose another group of five pupils and repeat the process with a new set of words. Before long, the entire class will be creating projects based upon stories of their own making. Who saw that on the cards?

Lost for words

It isn't often you can come up with a game that can be meted out as punishment for using bad language – but this is just that!

All you have to do is sentence anyone who speaks in an unfriendly manner to five minutes of mime. You're not strictly telling them just to be quiet, as they have to continue exactly whatever they were doing at the time, but they must now make themselves understood to both their fellow classmates and school staff without saying a single word.

Think of it as a verbal time-out with a creative edge. All you have to do is announce 'Five-minute mime!' to the guilty party, adding another minute for everything they say after sentence has been passed.

By the time they've flailed about, looking silly while they try to communicate, they'll have decided to watch their language for the rest of the day.

Speedy spell!

This is an action-packed game that involves some running around the classroom, so be sure to clear away any obstacles before you begin.

Split the room into boys and girls (or two teams if you're teaching a single-sex class) and choose one player from each side. Now, on your command, these two players must dash around the room and be the first to collect a specific item to bring back to you. The good news is that all the items are revealed through spelling clues!

Start simple, for example by announcing that you need an object that begins with the letter 'C'. Both players must now run to find a cup or a piece of chalk, etc. The rest of their team-mates can shout out encouragement, or even yell the location of a suitable item – but they must not leave their seats or collect any of the objects themselves.

Whichever player brings you an object that fits the clue stays in for the next round. The other player must, however, sit down and be replaced with one of their team-mates.

Here are a handful of suggested clues to use:

- Something that begins with the sixth letter of the alphabet
- Something that ends in 'T'
- Something that begins with a vowel
- Something that has two of the same letter
- Something that has the letter 'U' in it
- Something that has three letters
- Something that ends in 'ING'
- Something that begins with two letters after 'L'.

This activity is easily adapted for younger pupils who would not be able to follow the spelling clues. If you have a junior class, ask them to find these items:

- Something that is blue
- Something with a picture of an animal
- Something that teachers use
- Something you can eat
- Something made of wood
- Something that makes a noise
- Something that fits in your pocket
- Something you can wear.

Before long, the entire class will have tired legs and well-exercised brains!

Tell me about it

Another activity that encourages pupils to look at the language they use and, in particular, how they describe the world around them. It can be all too easy for children to refer to things they like as 'nice' and things they don't as 'rubbish' (or whatever the currently popular terms may be. At the time of writing, anything that provokes a positive response – from the latest toy to an afternoon's TV – is described in my area as being 'Mint!' I was rather taken aback when a friend of my son's informed me he'd bought some 'Mint trainers!' that weekend.)

Give each pupil a sheet of paper and a pen and ask them to describe an everyday item in the most outlandish and bizarre way they can. They could write about a car wash, portraying the rollers as the 'arms of the Incredible Hulk, gripping and consuming each car in turn' or even describe the classroom door as a 'white-painted portal to another realm'.

When they have finished (they only need to write a paragraph or two) they should exchange papers with one of their classmates who must rewrite the description, making it even more fantastical if they possibly can. Then, pass the piece on to a third pupil who must try to do the same.

Now, ask the original authors to stand and, in turn, read the finished description – without saying what it is they've written about. Will the rest of the class (besides their fellow authors) be able to work out what the subject is?

Award points for the most unusual or creative descriptions, and encourage the class to continue looking at everyday objects in this slightly skewed manner. You never know what they'll discover . . .

Alphabet chat

A quick word game that can be played anywhere (it's ideal for car or train journeys), but will stretch your pupils' word power to its limits!

Choose a subject for the game – such as 'Animals', 'Food' or 'Music' – then the class must have a conversation about that subject, taking it in turns to say a single sentence. Not too hard, you might think – but each sentence must begin with a consecutive letter of the alphabet.

For example, say you choose 'Animals', the first pupil should begin by saying something that starts with the letter 'A', maybe 'Ants are one of the strongest animals in the world!' The next pupil's task is to carry on the conversation (it must make sense), but their sentence must start with a 'B': 'But, they're very small and vulnerable to attack!'

The chat could proceed in this manner:

- 'Can you think of an animal that might attack ants?'
- 'Dogs have been known to eat them!'
- 'Eat them? That's disgusting!'
- 'Far more disgusting that what they usually eat!'
- 'Great Danes need to eat more than smaller dogs!'
- 'Hearty meals – that's what they need!'
- 'I know someone who owns a Great Dane!'

See if your class can keep the conversation going until they reach the final letter of the alphabet. They'll find that some letters are much tougher to use at the start of a sentence than others (you'll be amazed how a xylophone slips into almost every round of this game!).

Once your pupils have mastered this game, see if they can repeat the exercise, but this time running the alphabet in reverse – from 'Z' to 'A'. Once that becomes easy, ask them to begin each sentence with the same letter as their first name or – even – with everyone using the same letter over and over again!

A Beguiling Challenge, Designed Exclusively For Great Heroes!

Idea factory

To close this chapter, I'd like to introduce a couple of useful methods for generating story ideas. I'm including them because, whatever language your pupils are using – foul words, simple chatter or even flowery prose – it can be used to spark off classroom activities that the whole class can both enjoy and benefit from.

Let's take a couple of 'lower level' swear words: *bloody* and *damn*. In this example, I want you to imagine you have overheard one of your pupils using these words. You could come down hard on him or her, hand out a punishment or even send them off to explain themselves to the headteacher – or you can take what they've said and turn it into a learning exercise. (Of course, you should explain that you are not encouraging them to use such language for the purposes of education!)

Let's take the first word: *bloody*. Write it on the board and explain that, while it is commonly used as a swear word, it also has other meanings and contexts, and plenty of related words. Write some of these below the word, like this:

Bloody
Blood
Veins
Violent
Cut
Injury
Flesh
Accident
Hospital
Crime
Police

Now, do the same for the second word:

Damn
Water
Lake
Reservoir
Boat
Swimming
Bricks
Building
Power
Electricity
Energy

Ask your pupils to each choose one of the lower words from the first column, and one from the second, writing them together on a piece of paper. With any luck, the resulting pair of words will spark off an idea for a story.

In our example, the following pairs might appear (along with the suggested story idea in parentheses):

- *Blood boat* (The coastguard finds a boat floating at sea without anyone on board. On closer inspection, they discover the tiny cabin awash with blood and must piece together what happened to the boat's missing owner.)
- *Hospital bricks* (A man who is convinced that doctors who were treating his late wife were responsible for her death uses a digger to attack the walls of the hospital where they work. As the bricks begin to fall away, the race is on to save the patients before the building collapses.)
- *Violent water* (As a result of a heavy thunderstorm, a river bursts its banks and floods a tiny village in the middle of the night. The residents must try to rescue each other from the rising water as the storm continues to rage.)
- *Police power* (Crime is on the increase, and the government gives the police unlimited powers to deal with offenders in any way they see fit. Before long a culture of fear has developed as people fear the authorities who are supposed to protect them. How will the public react?)
- *Flesh reservoir* (Two friends go swimming in a local reservoir on a hot summer's day. While splashing about, they discover a human arm floating in the water. There is a ring on one of the swollen fingers, and a note clasped in the fist that reads: 'It's too late for me, but please help my sister! Don't go to the police, or they'll kill her'. The boys must turn detective to solve the grisly crime.)

Five very different storylines that your class can use to create a thrilling piece of creative writing – all because one of your pupils used bad language!

4 When push comes to shove

There are times when unruly behaviour turns physical and, no matter how hard you try to avoid it, pupils are pushed, pulled or even hit. The subject of personal space and when it is socially acceptable to manhandle another person is a complex one, and too lengthy to explore in detail within these pages. However, there are several drama exercises which I have found useful in demonstrating the effects of unwanted physical contact.

It is, of course, possible that violence in the classroom could be an indication that a child is receiving the same treatment at home. If you suspect this is the case (remembering that it could just as easily not be happening – a situation where an accusation could result in serious repercussions), please speak to your headteacher or school nurse for advice before proceeding.

The activities that follow involve children coming into contact with each other. These games must be supervised at all times, and can be used as a springboard to discuss situations when touching someone else is inappropriate.

Shark attack!

A game where one of your pupils must spot the shark before all the swimmers are attacked! Choose one of your pupils to be the shark hunter, and ask them to leave the room for a few moments. Next choose another pupil to be the shark, and make sure that everyone else knows who that person is. Then, ask the shark hunter to return.

Your classroom now becomes the sea, and the guests 'swim' in it by walking around, and moving their arms in a swimming stroke. The shark also does this to hide himself from the shark hunter, who simply walks around among the swimmers.

When the shark is ready – he attacks! He does this by gently squeezing one of the swimmer's legs. That swimmer must then continue swimming while counting up to five, then scream at the top of their voice, and drop to the seabed (fall to the floor!). All the swimmers then freeze for ten seconds while the shark hunter tries to guess who the shark is.

If he guesses correctly, the game is over, and another shark and hunter are chosen, but if he is wrong, the swimmers continue swimming, and the shark chooses another victim. Any victims lying on the floor should move out of the way, in case they get trodden on!

When the shark hunter finally spots the shark, pick another hunter to leave the room, and play again!

Club the caveman

Today, making friends often involves some kind of club. Back in prehistory, things were much the same!

Sit your pupils in a circle around a fire made from sticks and crepe paper (this is a good opportunity to remind them that you have made a fake fire, and never to play with the real thing), and blow up a long balloon to act as a club.

Your cave kids should cross their legs, close their eyes, and hold their hands in their laps with the palms facing up.

Wander around the circle in silence, reminding your class not to open their eyes. Eventually, choose one of them, gently place the club into their upturned hands, and keep on circling the group.

After a few seconds, shout 'Go clubbing!'. The player with the club must quickly choose the person either to their left or their right, and hit them on the head with the balloon. Both kids then jump up, and chase around the circle – clubbing all the while – while the rest of group open their eyes and chant 'Club! Club! Club!'

When both players reach their original spaces, they sit back down, and you take possession of the club again. All players must then fall silent, close their eyes, and wait for the next clubber to be picked.

There's nothing like a good bash!

Kiss kiss bang bang

Fighting isn't the only physical activity that may occur in your classroom. Kissing and affectionate touching can also be upsetting if uninvited. Here's a game that introduces the subject, allowing you to start a discussion with your pupils . . .

On a large sheet of paper (you could use the back of a length of wallpaper) draw three life-size babies. They don't have to be good drawings, just recognizable enough! Pin this paper at your pupils' head height to a wall, and clear any obstacles from in front of it.

Now, cut three sets of large lips from card (approximately 6cm in length) and paint them red. On the back of the lips, tape a 'V'-shaped piece of card so that it stands up like a handle. Place the lips down on a table, next to a saucer filled with PVA glue.

To play the game, each player is blindfolded in turn, and has one minute to grab a set of lips between their teeth, dip it in the glue, and use it to kiss the babies on the wall. Then they must find their way back to the table to get the other sets of lips, and repeat the kisses.

After all three sets of lips have been used, the blindfold is removed, and the player sees how well they have done. Award them ten points for a direct kiss on a baby's face, five for anywhere else on the body, and a bonus of five points if they managed to kiss all three babies.

Then, carefully remove the lips from the wall, blindfold the next player, and carry on kissing!

Up and atom

Of course, physical contact doesn't stop at fists – it's just as easy for a pupil to start throwing things around the classroom or, regrettably, at their classmates. In this activity, pupils must toss balls towards each other for a much more positive purpose. It does involve a little advance preparation but, once you have the props, you can keep them to play whenever you need to discourage target practice!

Stitch stripes of Velcro along the tops of two baseball caps. Use one side of the Velcro on one hat, and the opposite half on the other.

Next, get 20 or 30 table tennis balls, and stick patches of Velcro onto those at regular intervals (if you can't get ping pong balls, screw up sheets of newspaper as tightly as you can, and tape them in place.) Again, use one side of the Velcro on half of the balls, and the opposite side on the other.

Split the class into two teams, and get them to choose one of their players to be the nucleus of an atom. These two players step into the centre of the room, put their hands in their pockets, and each wears one of the Velcro-covered baseball caps. Divide the balls evenly between the two teams – these will be the protons.

To play the game, the two teams must throw the balls into the air above the two baseball-capped nuclei. They must duck under the shower of protons, and try to get as many of them to stick to the Velcro on their heads as possible. Only half of the balls will stick to each cap, so the game isn't quite as simple as it seems.

If a ball misses and falls to the floor, the nucleus can kick it back to his or her team-mates – but they mustn't take their hands out of their pockets, or touch the balls with any other part of their body.

As the game progresses, some attached protons will be dislodged by more falling particles, making play harder than ever.

When the time is up (two minutes is a good length for this experiment), the team with the highest number of protons stuck to their cap wins. Choose two more nuclei, swap the caps over, and play again.

An attractive game!

Secret squeeze

Stand your pupils in a circle and ask everyone to hold hands with the people on either side. Now, break the circle at one point and take hold of a pupil's hand. Squeeze that hand with a series of long and short grips – like a kind of a code. Perhaps you could give one long squeeze, followed by two short ones.

That pupil must now clench the hand of the next player along with exactly the same sequence of squeezes. Think of it as the old party favourite, Chinese Whispers, only with hand squeezes instead of whispered words.

Does the squeezed code remain the same all the way around the circle? If not, can you work out where things went wrong?

If you really want to have fun – try squeezing a word in actual Morse code. For example, the word 'drama' would be:

—.. .—. .— — .—

. . . where a full stop is a dot, or quick squeeze, and a hyphen is a dash, or longer squeeze. Make note of the sequence of dots and dashes at the end of the game and look up the letters here:

www.learnmorsecode.com

Just make sure it's suitable to read out before you tell your pupils!

Pass the pencil

This is a variation of an old party game which involves pupils passing an item around the classroom without using their hands. It can be used as an exercise to show that even brushing up against another person without permission can be considered inappropriate behaviour.

Arrange a number of general classroom items on desks around the room, such as pencils, books, pen pots and water bottles.

The pupil nearest to each of these items must choose one of them and pick it up without using their hands or their mouth. They can grip the item beneath their chin, between their arms, or even with their feet. They must now pass that item on to another pupil – who is also prohibited from using their hands or mouth – without dropping it on the floor. If an item is dropped, it is placed back in its starting position.

Once the second player has possession of the item, he or she must choose someone else to receive it while the original player goes back for another object. Before long, everyone in the class will be passing items around using different parts of his or her body.

Bubble burst

Personal space is a valuable commodity – just ask anyone who's stood with their face pressed into a stranger's armpit on a busy train journey! Here's an activity that explores the need for personal space in a fun way.

Ask your pupils to find a space to stand in (you may need to use the school hall or move some of the desks out of the way in the classroom). Explain to everyone that they should imagine themselves inside a bubble: a perfect sphere that completely surrounds them in every direction.

Now, just get on with your lessons for the day, but insist that no one should step within the boundaries of another person's bubble while moving around the classroom. If someone does invade your bubble, you must shout 'POP!' at the top of your voice to announce the fact.

When you first start playing this game, you'll hear a lot of popping but, as the activity continues, you'll discover that your pupils will become more aware of the space between themselves and their classmates and learn to respect it. Make it clear that you are not saying your pupils cannot be friendly towards each other, but simply that there are times when people need their personal space.

Touchy subject

The final exercise in this chapter involves the use of a blindfold, so be sure that your pupils are happy to have their eyes covered before you start the game.

Using a soft scarf, blindfold one of your pupils and stand them at the front of the class. Now, invite three of that person's friends to come and stand in front of them. Select one of the friends and tell the blindfolded pupil that they have 60 seconds to try and discover which of the three people it is by touch alone. The blindfolded player can feel the fabric of their friend's clothing (was the person they're looking for wearing a jumper or a T-shirt?). They can also feel the length and style of the other pupil's hair and judge their height from how much higher or lower their face is compared to their own.

After a minute, the blindfolded pupil must decide which one of the three people in front of them is the friend they're looking for and hold that person's hand. If they're right, award them some points.

Now, choose another pupil to wear the blindfold and get touchy all over again!

5 Musical youth

Some say that music is the food of love but, in this chapter, it'll be the quick snack of getting your pupils to do as you say!

Music, like drama, holds no prejudice. Whether you're a professional singer or a tone-deaf amateur, you can get the same enjoyment from listening to a piece of music as everyone else.

Music can also invoke emotions. Why else would they have a score to a movie, or add jingles to advertisements? The secret to using music to help keep order in the classroom is to tap into that emotive power and use it to your advantage.

Here are a couple of exercises that will show you how . . .

Please note: some of the following activities involve the use of copyrighted music on CD or in MP3 format. If you choose to run these exercises, your school will need to purchase a licence from the Performing Rights Society.

A licence is needed whether you use music in the classroom, hold a school disco or even play music over the telephone system while callers are on hold.

For more information, visit the Performing Rights Society at:

www.mcps-prs-alliance.co.uk

and the Centre for Education and Finance Management at:

www.cefm.co.uk

Pavlov's pupil

After abandoning a career as a priest, Ivan Petrovich Pavlov turned to science in 1870 and discovered a way to keep your classroom tidy. OK, there were a few steps in between, but that's going to be the end result.

In case you don't know of Pavlov's experiments, he realized that both animals and humans could be trained to react to certain stimuli. His most famous experiment – but by no means his only achievement – occurred when he began to ring a bell every time he fed his dogs. As soon as the dogs saw the food, they began to drool.

Before long, the dogs subconsciously associated the sound of the bell with the impending arrival of food and began to drool whether a meal was provided or not. This could be why the floor of your school dining room becomes wet shortly after the bell rings for lunch.

Pavlov went on to show that anyone could exhibit the same reaction to certain stimuli – so let's give it a go . . .

Choose an up-tempo piece of music, such as a song from the charts. Be aware, however, that you are likely to be playing this at least once a day, almost every day – so pick a song that won't drive you insane after the first three sessions!

Now, explain to your pupils that they have three minutes to tidy away what they're doing and get ready for the next lesson, and that you're going to play some music for them to enjoy while they're cleaning up. Start the song, and off they go.

Do the same thing the following day, and the two days after that – playing the same piece of music as your pupils tidy away whatever they've been using. On the fifth day, however, don't announce that it's time to tidy up, just play the music.

As they are now so used to tidying up to that particular song, many of your pupils will look to you to see if they are supposed to clear away. Encourage them to do so, saying that – if the music is playing – they should be tidying. You may need to offer the same encouragement that they are doing the right thing for a few more sessions but, before too long, all you'll have to do is switch on the music, and your class will spring into action.

If you want to change the piece of music at all, you'll have to begin all over again as your pupils won't associate this new song to the clearing up activity – and you may even find that they prefer the original tune (I warned you not to pick something you'd get tired of quickly!).

Now, if we can just find a song that will encourage them to do their homework . . .

One song disco

You know that feeling you get, just after lunch, when it seems that all your energy has somehow drained out of you and left an empty shell. Guess what? Your pupils feel it, too – they're just too stubborn to give in to it!

When I was acting in the West End musical *Buddy: The Buddy Holly Story*, we used to dread Friday coming around. On a Friday, we had two shows to perform: a matinee at 5.30 p.m. and an evening show at 8.30 p.m. As the show was 2 hours and 40 minutes in length, that meant we had 20 minutes between shows – just enough time to get out of one costume and into another to start all over again.

The problem was that we were frequently drained from the first show, and needed a boost as we went into the second. So, we invented the One Song Disco – something I've used with my drama classes ever since to provide instant energy whenever you need it. Try it out, and your afternoons will never drag again!

Choose an up-tempo song that you know your pupils will enjoy (unlike the previous activity, however, you can choose a different song every day). Now, gather everyone together in one area of the room.

Play the song as loud as you can (without disturbing other classes, of course!) and instruct everyone to dance as wildly as they can for the entire duration of the song. That's everyone – including you!

So long as everyone puts plenty of effort into their dancing, the song will end with everyone out of breath – but with no sign of the afternoon blues in sight. You'll now find that your pupils are wide-eyed and ready to learn whatever subject you want to teach next. Dance-tastic!

Relax!

Of course, there are times when you want your pupils to wind down and not be frothing with energy – and music can help you achieve that, too. You'll need a softer, more gentle piece of music for this exercise. Perhaps even a classical track.

If you have room, ask your pupils to find a space on the floor where they can lie down and close their eyes. If you don't have room to do that, ask everyone to fold their arms on their desks and rest their heads forward, again with eyes closed.

Now, play the gentle music and ask everyone to breathe deeply. You may get some giggles the first few times you run the exercise, but they'll stop as soon as everyone realizes how much better they feel after a few minutes of relaxation.

You can add to the atmosphere of serenity by reading out a short story or a description of a comforting place while the music plays, asking everyone to picture what you're saying in their minds.

Try reading something like the following (although you can write your own version if you like), pausing for a few seconds between each paragraph to allow the images to solidify in your pupils' imaginations.

Note: for those who may be concerned, this is not hypnosis in any form. Gentle music and comforting words are simply used to help your pupils to experience a sensation of relaxation they may not otherwise get at school. However, if you have any doubts, please do not run this exercise.

Suggested relaxation script

'Close your eyes and take a deep breath. Hold it for a second, then breathe out slowly. Take another deep breath in, hold it, now breathe out slowly . . .

'I want you to imagine you step through the classroom door and find yourself on a beach in the sunshine. You've taken your shoes off, and the sand feels warm between your toes. The sea is calm and washes quietly in and out beside you. Let's go for a walk along the beach . . .

'Up above you the sky is blue, and the few clouds you can see are fluffy and white. Birds fly overhead and sing out their calls. Butterflies settle on the flowers that run along the edge of the beach . . .

'You come across a wooden box in the sand – shaped like a pirate chest – and you open its lids to find that it's empty. Now, we're going to use this box to get rid of any bad feelings we've had this week . . .

'I want you to think of any time that you were angry or upset at school over the past few days. Perhaps you were cross with one of your friends, or frustrated that you couldn't do something as well as you'd hoped. Think about how that situation made you feel . . .

'Now, take those feelings and drop them into the box. Make sure they all go in; you don't want to miss any. Now, shut the lid on the box and close the lock . . .

'Beside the box you find a spade, and begin to dig a deep hole in the sand. When the hole is deep enough, you drop the box inside and cover it with sand. We're not going to let those feelings bother us again . . .

'Now, we're walking back along the beach towards the classroom. Getting closer and closer . . . You step back into the classroom and sit at your desk (or lie down on the carpet, whichever your pupils are doing). Now, you take another deep breath, hold it for a second, then let it out. Open your eyes and sit up . . .'

Fade the music out as everyone opens their eyes and sits up, making sure that none of your pupils have fallen asleep during the exercise (if any have, wake the sleepers gently and reassure them, as they may be embarrassed).

Now you can continue with the day's lessons content that everyone is feeling relaxed, refreshed and raring to go!

Radio ga ga

A great way to use music and drama together in an activity that promotes teamwork is to start your own class radio station. Everyone must work together to make sure the broadcast is a success.

The first thing to do is to distribute jobs. You could pick names out of a hat for each position, ask for volunteers, or even have your pupils attend a mock interview for the job they're after.

Some of the positions you need to fill are:

DJ

The DJ will be recording his or her voice as the presenter of the radio show. There can, of course, be more than one DJ. You might decide to go with a male/female pairing or – like many breakfast radio shows – employ what is sometimes known as a ringmaster style, where one main DJ talks to and plays off a number of assistants in the studio.

The pupils chosen to speak on air should practise talking clearly and slowly (they'll be amazed how fast and garbled everything sounds when they first hear their voices back on tape).

Production team

These pupils have the challenging task of gathering together everything that is needed for the show. They'll need to: choose the songs that will be played and make sure the CDs are available; write competition questions and locate prizes; ensure that the running order is followed and that the timing of the show is adhered to; and write the DJ's script, if there is to be one.

You'll need to choose pupils with a certain amount of common sense to join the production team: there's nothing worse than being live 'on air' and finding that you have the wrong CD or the quiz questions are missing!

Newsreader

In most modern radio newsrooms, the newsreader is also the person who gathers the stories for the news bulletin and writes the script. You'll need a pupil with an eye for a good story as they'll need to scour the local papers and search the internet for topics that will be of interest to your listeners.

Your newsreader will also need a calm, clear voice that expresses the serious nature of the stories; you don't want someone giggling halfway through an item about a missing pet.

Sports reporter

Like the newsreader, the sports reporter will need to find the top stories and write them into a script that can be read on air in a clear voice.

Jingle singers

These pupils will need to write a snappy station jingle, and record themselves singing it together (with the help of the engineers). They should listen to their local radio station to get an idea of what a jingle sounds like, then make one up of their own (they don't need backing music – the jingle can be sung a cappella, without instruments).

The other option is for the singers to perform the jingle live during the show. There is more room for error that way, but the final ident will have much more energy!

Traffic reporter

Unlike the newsreader and sports reporter, the person in charge of traffic is likely to have to invent their entire report (after all, roadworks and contraflows are of little interest to the average school pupil who might listen to the show). So, they can have some fun with details of a dinner lady pile-up outside the secretary's office, or giving a warning of a slow moving toddler near the nursery.

Editors

The editors are the pupils who will take the raw footage recorded by the on-air presenters, and assemble it into a final show. If you're recording the show onto a computer (details of exactly how to do that follow) they'll need some prior knowledge of how to use a PC. If you're recording the old-fashioned way – onto tape – they'll need to be quick on the pause button!

Engineers

Again, what your radio station's engineers need to know depends on how you will be recording your show. If, as I recommend, you record directly onto a computer, they'll need to be able to set up a microphone and provide some sort of soundproofing (the best way to do this is to stand chairs on tables and surround those speaking on air with heavy blankets).

PR department

What good is a radio station if no one listens to it? While you won't actually be broadcasting your show on the air, your publicity department will need to act as though you are by designing a logo for the station, taking presenters' photographs and writing their biographies and preparing a press release to let the world know when the show itself will happen.

Perhaps your PR team could even design a website for the station? They don't need to do it on a computer (although if they can – fantastic!) as almost all websites start off as drawings on paper in their early stages.

Advertising team

Advertising is the lifeblood of radio. Listen to any local station and you'll hear advert breaks roughly every 20 minutes. Most stations have huge sales teams that telephone local businesses and pitch the advantages of advertising on radio – although your ad-mad pupils will have things a little easier.

Your advertising team should either choose a couple of local shops to advertise during the show or make up a business or two that might need the boost of being promoted on air. Next, they need to write a short script – almost like a comedy sketch – that sets out a problem suffered by a potential customer and is solved by the business. As anyone who's ever worked in advertising will tell you – this isn't an easy task, and so you'll need some of your most creative pupils in this department.

When a script is finally ready, the advertising team should contact the jingle singers to get their musical input and then hire a group of . . .

Actors

This final group will be performing the scripts prepared and written by the advertising team. Make sure you have plenty of talent in this group – as they'll need to portray a variety of characters in a short space of time.

Once everyone has a job, it's time to hold your first production meeting. First of all, decide upon a name for your radio station. Maybe you could use part of the class or school name? If that doesn't sound right, try the name of the road the school is in, or even make up a totally new word! It just has to be something the listeners will remember.

Now you can put together a running order for your first show, including which songs you're going to play, when the news and weather are read and which, if any, competitions you're going to run. You also need to work out roughly how long each segment will last.

A sample running order could look like this:

Drama Radio – Running Order

1   Jingle and station ID (30 seconds)
2   Introduction from the DJ (3 minutes)
3   Song 1 – current chart hit (3 minutes)
4   Adverts (1.5 minutes)
5   Intro to news by DJ (30 seconds)
6   News report (3 minutes)
7   Weather (2 minutes)
8   Jingle and station ID (30 seconds)
9   Song 2 – favourite from last summer (3 minutes)
10   Competition by DJ (4 minutes)
11 Traffic report (1 minute)
12 Adverts (1.5 minutes)
13 Song 3 – current chart hit (3 minutes)
14 Goodbye from DJ (3 minutes)
15 Jingle and station ID (30 seconds).

Sticking to this running order would result in a 30-minute long radio show. Perfect for a first attempt. Now it's time to record – but how?

The technique I recommend for creating your radio show is to record directly onto a computer. To do this, you'll need several things:

1   A PC with plenty of space on the hard drive (recording takes up a lot of room)
2   A microphone to plug into the PC
3   Sound-recording software.

Fortunately, the recording software is the least of your problems, as a superb program called Audacity can be downloaded for free from:

http://audacity.sourceforge.net/

Have the pupils you've chosen to be editors play around with the software for a while, so they can get used to cutting, copying and pasting the sections into a specific order. They can also import different files – such as songs in MP3 format or sound effects – to include in the show. Search the internet for tutorials on how to get the most out of Audacity.

If your PC isn't up to the job, you'll need to resort to good old tape. Simply record everything for your show onto cassette in the order you need it, then connect the player up to another cassette deck to edit out the gaps with the pause button (just like making mix-tapes when we were young and in love!).

When your radio show is complete, you can gather pupils together to listen to the finished product, although, if you intend to make copies of the programme to give out, you'll need a different kind of licence from the Performing Rights Society.

Group 4

Musical Chairs is dead. Write that down and repeat it every day. In fact, if you take nothing else away from this book other that that phrase, the time I spent to write it will have been worthwhile. (And no, you can't get away with Musical Statues or Musical Bumps, either).

You may ask why – after all the game is played at virtually every birthday party, school get-together and play meeting that's ever held. The reason is simple: you're the one who's going to have to cope with a dozen bored-out-of-their-mind kids while two determined finalists battle it out over the final chair.

As I explained in the introduction to this book – running any game where children are 'out' at any point is just asking for trouble. While you're working hard to entertain those still playing, the rest are seeing who can stuff the class gerbil into their mouths or tearing up the carpet in search of an entrance to Narnia. OK, maybe that's an exaggeration – but you get the idea.

Much better to play a musical game where everyone stays in and playing from start to finish – and I've got just the thing in Group 4 . . .

Ask everyone to find a space and play a song, as you would for any of the musical games mentioned above. The difference is that, when you stop the music, you have to shout out a number – 1, 2, 3 or 4 – and your pupils must get themselves into groups of that size as quickly as they can. If you have a class of exactly 12, 24 or 36 pupils, everyone will be able to join a group. If not, simply hit play again and everyone goes back to dancing by themselves – no one is out, or left to feel that they've lost in any way.

Once your pupils are used to the game, try shouting higher numbers such as 5, 9 or 13 to see how quickly they can arrange themselves into groups. You could even throw a sneaky bit of maths in there, too – announcing that they need to be in groups of '12 minus 5' or '18 divided by 2'.

You can easily adapt this game for younger players, too. Just switch from numbers to nature and, whenever the music stops, call out the name of an animal. The players must immediately pretend to be that creature and make the correct animal sounds – eventually collapsing into giggles when you shout out that everyone must become a worm!

Musical Chairs is dead. Let it rest in peace.

Rhyme time

Some of the first songs we ever learn are nursery rhymes. But have your pupils ever stopped to think about what really happened to Humpty Dumpty, or why the Grand Old Duke of York was so keen on keeping his men moving at all times? Here's a way to use drama to explore the simplest of songs.

Write the names of several nursery rhymes onto pieces of card. Some of the best ones to use for this activity include:

- 'Hey Diddle Diddle'
- 'Wee Willie Winkie'
- 'Humpty Dumpty'
- 'The Grand Old Duke Of York'
- 'Three Blind Mice'
- 'Jack and Jill'.

Split your class into groups of five or six pupils and then ask each group to choose a card at random. Once they have their nursery rhyme – it's time to act. Your pupils will have 20 minutes to invent a short play about the rhyme.

They should begin by working out who will be playing which character. There are some rhymes which only feature one or two people – such as 'Wee Willie Winkie'

– but explain to your class that they are allowed to invent new characters if they wish.

If you're working with younger pupils, the pieces they put together will be relatively straightforward, following the plot of the rhyme to the letter (you may have to remind them of exactly what happens by singing the nursery rhyme together first).

However, if your class is old enough, they can really have some fun. Ask them to bring their rhymes right up to date, and to explore any secrets in the story that children's books have kept hidden.

For example, they may decide that Humpty Dumpty was a trouble-making teen, always hanging out on people's garden walls shouting abuse and hurling insults. Maybe he was pushed from the wall by a passer-by who didn't like being called a rude name and, when the King's horses and King's men finally showed up, they didn't put him back together as they figured the kingdom was better off without the yolk-filled lout.

In the story of 'Hey Diddle Diddle' – did the cow really jump over the moon of her own free will, or was she launched there by the dog who'd do just about anything for laughs? Was the cat playing a mournful song on his fiddle as the cow re-entered the Earth's atmosphere, and did the dish and the spoon run away to avoid being crushed as the cow hit the ground?

Once each group has worked out what happens in their story and who will be playing who, it's time for them to rehearse. Their play doesn't need to be long – one or two minutes is perfect. Explain that they should remember where the audience will be sitting, and to make sure that they are facing in that direction when they perform. They should also try not to all speak at the same time – it can make even the easiest rhyme difficult to understand!

When the time is up, sit everyone down together on one side of the room, then ask each group in turn to perform their play. Encourage everyone in the audience to clap at the end of each piece, and you could even ask a few questions about the way the story was acted out.

If you want to tackle a bigger play project – check out the script of *Aladdin* at the end of this book!

Vocal warm-up

The final few activities in this chapter involve your pupils – and you – making use of your voices (don't worry, I won't be making you sing solo in front of everyone; I'll let you save that for the staff karaoke night out!).

The voice is an instrument, plain and simple and, like all instruments, it has to be cared for if it is to make the sounds you want it to make. Here is a simple vocal warm-up that you can use with your class. Not only will it help to exercise their diaphragms and vocal chords, but it will also develop their lung capacity – perfect for those playtimes when all they do is run around.

Ask your pupils to find a space and stand in it with their legs slightly apart and their arms hanging loosely at their sides. Now, you're going to ask them to breathe (a seemingly pointless command as they do it all the time – but you'd be amazed how many of your pupils have never thought about their own breathing before).

Note: it is possible that one or more of your pupils could become light-headed as a result of this exercise. This is down to hyperventilating and is nothing serious. If it happens, ask that pupil to sit down and breathe normally until they feel better.

To begin the exercise, explain to your pupils that you want them to take a deep breath for the count of four, hold that breath inside for the count of four, and then breathe out for a further count of four. At the end of the final four, they need to have expelled all the air in their lungs. Count your class through this section by saying out loud:

> In, two, three, four . . .
> Hold, two, three, four . . .
> Out, two, three, four . . .

Repeat this a couple of times until everyone is comfortable with following the instructions. Now, it's time to work that breath!

This time, you're going to repeat the exercise, but ask everyone to breathe in for the count of eight, hold for four, then breathe out to the count of eight:

> In, two, three, four, five, six, seven, eight . . .
> Hold, two, three, four . . .
> Out, two, three, four, five, six, seven, eight . . .

Your pupils will discover that they are now having to think about their breathing as they are trying to expel all the air in their lungs by the end of the count to eight. One or two of them will run out of breath before you reach the number five – and a few will have timed it wrong, and have to blow out the last puff of air after you've finished speaking. Repeat this section until everyone can breathe out smoothly to the count of eight.

The next stage of the warm-up exercises your pupils' vocal chords as well as their lung capacity. They're going to breathe in for a count of eight again, hold their breath for a count of four but, this time, they're going to count out loud to eight, instead of just breathing out. So:

(You) In, two, three, four, five, six, seven, eight . . .
(You) Hold, two, three, four . . .
(All) One, two, three, four, five, six, seven, eight . . .

Explain that the idea is to have run out of breath by the time they are saying the number eight. It will take some practice but, after a few tries, everyone should be able to manage it.

If you repeat this vocal warm-up – say, once or twice a week – you'll find that counting to eight on the last breath becomes easy and is no longer a challenge. When this happens, try increasing the number your pupils have to count to with the same amount of breath. They'll soon be able to reach 12, 16 and even 20. This will be doing them good, too, as there is considerable evidence that breathing out for extended but comfortable periods stimulates the lymphatic system, helping the body to remove impurities.

Now your pupils are warmed-up to warble . . .

Going for a song

Every year, on Christmas Eve, I would take my mum to Midnight Mass. And, every year, on Christmas Eve, the parish priest at our local church would sing Midnight Mass. Not just the hymns, but the entire Mass. Every single word.

The effect was incredible. The congregation, used to settling down for a snooze while they anticipated the following day's festivities, now sat upright and listened to every note – entranced by the haunting sound of the priest's voice echoing around the church.

It got me thinking (after Mass had ended, of course) about the way I taught my drama lessons. Would it be possible to teach an entire class in song? And could the children be encouraged to ask for information and answer questions in the same way? Nervously, I tried it – and the results were incredible!

Now, before I go any further – I am not a singer. I may have spent a good portion of my career in stage musicals but, although I enjoy a good karaoke session as much as the next man, I was never awarded any of the roles where the ability to belt out a tune counted. I was given the speaking parts every time. So don't worry about singing in front of your pupils. They're not expecting Pavarotti!

Choose the lesson you're going to try this with very carefully. You may find it fun to sing out facts concerning the ice age, but crooning your way through the industrial revolution is going to be a lot tougher!

Once you have chosen a subject you have a choice: you can either use a tune your pupils will be familiar with, or you can just 'busk' the lesson and simply transform your speech by making it more musical. Whichever way you decide to go, I would advise starting off the lesson like this:

Do not tell your pupils you're about to sing!

Why? Quite simply because, if they weren't sitting up and paying attention up until that moment – they are now! If you have a particularly astute class, they may cotton on to the exercise themselves and begin to sing questions to you straight away. If not, don't worry, they just need a little encouragement to join in.

You don't have to run this exercise for long – a 15-minute sung question and answer session about the current topic is enough for anyone. You will, however, discover that your pupils have retained just about every fact you sang to them – quite simply because they will be able to associate the tune to the information when thinking back over the lesson.

If you pick one subject a week and sing it, not only will your pupils look forward to their musical moments, but you'll receive the most awe-inspired glances the staff room has ever seen!

Waxing lyrical

An ideal follow on to the previous activity is to ask your class to invent their own lyrics to their favourite songs. Not only is this a valuable creative writing exercise, but you'll find that even the most unruly of pupils will simmer down if they're allowed to bring their own CDs into school.

As always, I have to remind you that playing music in the classroom – even for educational purposes – requires a licence from the Performing Rights Society. See the beginning of this chapter for details of how to apply.

To run the activity, ask your pupils to write down the lyrics from one of their favourite songs. If they have the CD, but can't quite make out what's being sung, a quick search of the internet should result in a version of the lyrics they can print off.

Once they have the original words, it's time to rewrite them – making the new lyrics as funny as possible. For example . . .

> I'm going to insert a small author's note here. Writers are very wary of including references to pop culture in their books. Manuscripts are written well in advance of publication dates and, by the time the book hits the shelves, the song mentioned could already be long forgotten, dating the book terribly. With this in mind, we'll be travelling back in time to 1999 for our example, when Robbie Williams released his single, 'She's The One'. After all, you can't date an old song . . .

Have a listen to the original lyrics – all about finding someone special (and other things your pupils will think is yucky). However, with a little creative writing, they can become:

> My dad's hair
> Used to be
> On his head
> Just like me
> Now his head's shiny
> No hair left on
> It's all gone.

See what your pupils can do with their own CDs, singing their new words over the original songs. If they're anything like those my own son is currently listening to, it can only be an improvement!

Movers and shakers

Now that your pupils have got used to singing in the classroom it's time to add some music to the mix – and the best part is, making your own musical instruments is a fantastic classroom activity!

Everyone knows how easy it is to make a shaker by pouring rice inside a yoghurt pot and replacing the lid (then sealing it tightly with tape after you've picked all the rice back up from the carpet two minutes later), but here are a couple of ideas for musical makes that may be new to you . . .

You can make a kazoo with nothing more than an old toilet roll tube, an elastic band and a piece of tissue paper (I knew I'd get the opportunity to go all 'Blue Peter' on you!).

All your pupils have to do is take the tube from the middle of a toilet roll or kitchen roll, and paint it to make it look a little more attractive. When the paint is dry, they should use a pencil to poke two or three holes along the side of the tube (the kazoo won't work if they don't make these holes, so ensure they don't skip this part).

Finally, secure a piece of tissue paper over one end of the tube with an elastic band and – hey presto – you have a great sounding kazoo whenever you hum into the other end of the tube!

Another fun instrument to make is a water xylophone. For this, however, you'll need a selection of glass bottles in the classroom, so it may not be a suitable activity for younger pupils.

Collect together eight empty glass bottles and try hitting them with pencils. They'll each make a ringing sound, a bit like the musical note you hear when a xylophone is played. However, it's unlikely you'll be able to get much of a song out of this set-up – unless you tune it . . .

By adding water to each of the bottles, you can change the note it produces when you hit it with a pencil. It will take a little experimentation to get the notes to sound right – adding or removing a tiny bit of water at a time. However, by the time you've finished, you should be able to play any number of musical melodies!

Once you have your instruments assembled (including all the shakers your class can handle), see if you can perform together as an orchestra. You'll find it's a good idea to start off by playing a simple tune, such as 'Baa Baa Black Sheep' and make your way up to Vivaldi's *Four Seasons* when you've had time to practise!

Any pupils without an instrument can use their voices to form a chorus – so long as you make allowances for the odd cough or burp halfway through your recital!

Part Two
STAGING A PANTOMIME TO ENCOURAGE TEAMWORK

6 Let's do the show right here!

While most of the exercises and activities in the book are aimed specifically at controlling behaviour in the classroom, your pupils will always enjoy taking part in drama simply for drama's sake. Sadly as fewer and fewer schools are able to include the subject in their curriculum, many pupils never get the chance to appear on stage, whether for the benefit of their friends, teachers or parents.

With this in mind, I have decided to fill the second half of this book with a major drama project – a whole play. A pantomime, in fact. The last chapter – Chapter 7 – features an original script I've written for the pantomime *Aladdin*.

The benefits of staging a play as a class project are numerous. Team work and cooperation are required in order to prepare the show, and reading and communication skills are used in the learning and delivering of lines. Memory is exercised by practising and remembering songs and dance routines. Plus, there are costumes to make, props to build and scenery to paint. Everyone takes part, and everyone works together to produce a final product which you can show to the rest of the school, or even perform for friends and family.

Don't worry if you've never produced or directed a play before – I'm going to tell you exactly what you need to do, broken down into each individual section required for the project. Just remember that there is no 'right' or 'wrong' when putting on a play; if you decide to do 'Aladdin In Space' – go for it. You want your characters to wear fluorescent pyjamas? Great idea! So long as everyone is having fun!

So, roll up your showbiz sleeves, and let's get to work!

The script

Everything starts with the script, so the Hollywood saying goes. While this may not be tinsel town, the script is still the most important part of your play – and I've written one especially for you.

In the final chapter of this book is a complete two-act script for an *Aladdin* pantomime – and it's yours to tweak however you want. Don't like some of the gags? Cut them! Want to change the Princess's name to Ethel? Go right ahead! Don't want songs in your show? Drop them!

How you alter and use the script is up to you. You can cut it down so you can perform the whole thing in half an hour, or add a third act to make it even longer. The only thing I ask is that you don't try to sell it as your own work on eBay, and that you consider giving me the writing credit in your panto programme!

Now, I've worked with scripts in book form myself and, quite frankly, they're a pain. So – to help you out – I've put the entire thing in rich text format on the Continuum Books website:

www.continuumbooks.com/resources/9781855394469

You can download this version to your favourite word processor, adapt it as necessary, then print off as many copies as you need. Unlike commercially purchased scripts, you can perform this without paying me a single penny in royalties, and there are no limits to the number of times you can raise the curtain.

Don't have word processing software on your computer with which to rework the script? No problem, you can download the superb Open Office suite for free from this address:

www.openoffice.org

I'm not affiliated with the site in any way, and I don't get any sort of commission from them. This is simply good, free software that will help you change the *Aladdin* script to suit your needs.

We have a script – now we need some actors . . .

Casting

The simplest way to cast your pantomime is to hold auditions for anyone who wants to play a part. While that may sound like a nightmare to organize, it's really not too difficult.

Ask anyone who wants to audition to memorize a page from a children's book (at least 100 words in length) and to practise singing a nursery rhyme. The idea of learning an entire page may seem daunting to some of your pupils but, if they can't memorize 100 words, they won't remember an entire script full of lines. It's a good first step to narrowing down your choices.

For those who do memorize a page from a book, ask them to recite it for you one at a time, putting as much emotion and excitement into the piece as possible. This may be something you want to do at lunchtime or after school when you can invite pupils into the classroom one at a time, although – I hate to say it – if they can't act in front of their friends, how are they going to be with an audience of strangers?

You'll also need to hear your potential performers sing their nursery rhyme without musical backing. Don't worry too much about finding a perfect singer (this *is* just a school play after all), but it will need your leading actors to be able to carry a tune and stick to the words.

Keep the list of characters beside you while listening to the recitals, bearing in mind the type of person you're looking for to play each part:

Aladdin

A boy with a good personality and a clear voice (don't be tempted to go down the traditional girl playing the principal boy route – the resulting love-song scenes make parents feel understandably uncomfortable).

Princess Blossom

A girl with a good personality and a clear voice – and someone who doesn't mind holding hands with whoever you cast as Aladdin! Trust me – I've seen entire productions go down the chute because the leading boy and leading girl wouldn't stand within two metres of each other!

Wishee Washee

A boy with a great sense of humour and comic timing.

Widow Twankey

This is one tradition you can stick to. Yes, you can cast a girl as the pantomime dame but, if there's a boy brave enough to strap on the dress and wear a ridiculous wig, he will become the star of the show – guaranteed!

Abanazer

A boy with the ability to look mean while being taunted by the audience. It's not as easy as it sounds!

Chop and Suey

The police officers can be boys or girls and, as with Wishee, you're looking for a pair with good comic timing.

The Genie

Boy or girl, someone brimming with confidence.

Slave of the Ring

Boy or girl – another fun personality needed here.

Emperor

A boy (or you can just as easily have an Empress) with an air of authority about them. In some productions, it is traditional for the director to play the Emperor – so why not have a go yourself?

Rose, Daisy, Pansy

Small but important roles. The handmaidens are the Princess's equivalent of Wishee Washee, so you'll need girls with a sense of humour.

Townspeople, extra policemen, spirits, dancers

These characters don't have any lines, and so are perfectly suited to those pupils who want to appear on stage but don't have the courage to speak or, as is sometimes the case, make about as much noise as a sleeping mouse.

It may also be a good idea to line up some understudies to the main parts of the show. An understudy is someone who steps into the role at the last moment if the actor cannot perform due to illness or unavailability and is, unfortunately, a thankless task. Understudies must learn the main actor's lines, songs and dance routines – and chances are that they won't get to perform them on stage. However, you'll thank yourself if you have someone to play Abanazer because the boy lined up to play the bad guy broke his arm in PE that morning!

One way to reward the understudies is to arrange an additional performance of the play with these hard-working pupils playing the roles they have rehearsed just in case. That way, their parents and friends can come along and watch their moment in the limelight.

There are, of course, plenty of jobs to be had for pupils who may not want to appear on stage. Those pupils will be busy with tasks such as these . . .

Costumes

Costumes can be expensive to hire or buy – which is why making your own is always a good idea. The good news is that costumes for *Aladdin* can be made from old items of clothing donated from home, or purchased from charity shops.

The overall look for the show is ancient Chinese – which can be achieved by wearing oversized, adult shirts with the collars cut off and plain leggings. Search online for examples of Chinese writing, then draw a symbol onto each shirt with bright fabric paint to customize the shirts. These costumes will be ideal for the townspeople and dancers.

Aladdin usually wears a colourful waistcoat and baggy trousers with his shirt. You can make the waistcoat by removing the sleeves from a bright T-shirt, then cutting it open at the front. Make the trousers by taking a long skirt and sewing a line up the centre – to about two-thirds of the way to the waistband, making the two separate sections that act as trouser legs.

As Aladdin comes from a poor family, stitch some large, colourful patches onto his costume. To show the change in lifestyle when he becomes a Prince, make a similar costume, but this time cover it with sequins and gold braid.

Make Wishee Washee and Abanazer's costumes in the same way, choosing suitable colours and patterns. If you can, make Abanazer a long cape from dark or black material so that he can dramatically sweep it aside when he walks!

For the Genie, Slave of the Ring and the spirits, choose lighter materials and add plenty of sequins to catch the light. Large blue shirts with toy sheriff's badges pinned to the front will work for Chop and Suey, the police officers.

Finally, make Widow Twankey's costume as bright and gaudy as possible! Layer skirts over the top of each other to give a bustle effect and, if you can get one, a ridiculous wig will complete the look.

Now it's time to add the greasepaint . . .

Make-up

Some of the boys (or even girls) may feel self-conscious about wearing make-up, so, unless you're performing in a venue with powerful lighting, it may be better to keep this to a bare minimum.

If you do have strong lights, they might wash the colour from your performer's cheeks and make their eyes difficult to see. This can be remedied by applying a thin coat of a flesh-coloured base or pancake over the face and a thin black pencil line beneath each eye.

Wishee Washee always looks great with over-the-top rosy cheeks and a nose covered with freckles. Darken Abanazer's eyebrows with black eye pencil and give him a sharp, little goatee beard. As for Widow Twankey . . . bright, clashing colours for the eyes are the order of the day. For the mouth, apply bright red lipstick in an 'M' shape above the top lip, and a 'W' below the bottom lip.

To get more ideas for stage make-up, a quick search of the internet will prove invaluable. You'll even find pictures of me in various panto guises (including Abanazer and a Twankey-style Ugly Sister) on the gallery page of my website:

www.tommydonbavand.com/gallery

Scenery

When staging any production, the temptation to really go to town with the scenery can be great. Yet, a simple set with a few colourful extras can be just as effective as busy stage decoration.

Try covering the back wall of your performance area with plain white sheets (these can be picked up very cheaply from your nearest big supermarket) and painting large Chinese symbols onto them in bright or even fluorescent paint. If sheets aren't an option, you can use rolls of wallpaper, pinning up lengths so that the plain back of the paper is showing, ready to paint.

On either side of the performance space, you'll need to create an off-stage area

– known in the theatre as the wings. These areas are where your pupils will go when they step off stage to change their costume or collect a prop, and they are relatively simple to make. One way is to use a free-standing clothes rail, over which you hang a curtain or length of dark-coloured cloth. You can also fix a broom handle onto a wall bracket and hang the curtain that way.

You will find your performance runs a lot smoother if you are able to move any performers from the wing space and into a nearby classroom when they're not required on stage. The wings can very quickly become cramped if there are lots of people milling about, and it can be difficult to keep everyone quiet. If you can construct your wing space so that it covers a doorway to a classroom or corridor, you will be saving yourself a lot of headaches!

Finally, you may require a cross-over area to get actors from one side of the stage to the other without being seen. If you have a corridor that runs behind your performance area, this is ideal. If you don't, and everyone has to come back onto the stage from the same side they last exited to – you'll need to remember this when directing the play.

Of course, if you want to build a more complicated set, there's nothing to stop you. Making wooden frames and stretching a durable canvas across them isn't the easiest job in the world (the reason that all theatre companies employ set designers and builders), but it's certainly nothing that's beyond the scope of your local carpenter or handyman.

If you do decide to use free-standing sections of set (known as flats), make sure they are all properly weighted down and cannot fall and injure anyone. Also, take great care when carrying them in and out of your performance area, insisting that two people carry each flat at all times, no matter how small or light they are. It's very easy to walk into someone while carrying a piece of scenery, or to turn sharply and hurt one of your fellow performers. Safety always comes first.

Now, if you add a few simple shapes cut from card and made so that that they can stand up by themselves (glue an L-shaped shelf bracket upside down to the back and rest a weight or brick onto it), your set will really come to life. You could cut out and paint a few market stalls for the scenes in Old Pekin, or distant pyramids for when Abanazer first summons the Slave of the Ring.

If you construct a large rock, either by cutting one from flat card or by building the shape from wire mesh and covering it with paper mâché, you have the entrance to the Cave of Wonders. Abanazer can slide this to one side to open the cave, then trap Aladdin inside in order to trap him there.

To make the inside of the Cave of Wonders look effective – you need props . . .

Props

Props is short for properties and, in the world of theatre, this means everything the actors carry or use on stage, or anything that is used to decorate or 'dress' the set. Making props is a superb class activity, and it's something that can be done over a period of time as you lead up to your performance.

To decorate your Cave of Wonders scene, gather together as many basic items as you can – then spray them all with gold paint (making sure to choose a well-ventilated area and to wear a mask over your mouth and nose). You will be amazed how different a set of plastic picnic plates or a battered old lamp looks when sprayed gold. Add as many items as you can find that look like jewels (raid charity shops for bangles and necklaces you can stick sequins to), and you have everything for the spirits to carry on and lay at Aladdin's feet as the Genie transforms him to a Prince.

There is also a scene in the script where everyone whizzes around on flying carpets and, while these are a little more difficult to make, will guarantee applause as soon as they appear. For each magic carpet, you'll need a sheet of hardboard or plywood with a hole cut in the middle (the hole must be big enough for your actors to fit through, as they'll be running around, carrying the 'carpets' during the chase).

Cover the sheets of wood with bright material, adding fringes at either end or tassels to the corners to make them look like rugs. Now, cut the legs from an old pair of trousers and fill them with old rags or the stuffing you can get to make cuddly toys. Sew a slipper at the end of each leg, and fasten the limbs to either side of the hole in the magic carpet.

If you make the fake legs similar to the costumes the various characters are wearing, the actors can wear black leggings and run around the stage, looking as though they are flying on the carpets. It doesn't matter that everyone in the audience will be able to see that the legs dangling over the sides are fake – in fact, it's likely to add to the comic value of the scene!

For Twankey's laundry, fill washing baskets with piles of old clothes and stick a sink plunger onto the end of a broom handle to make the stirrer used by Wishee Washee. The washing line that's wound round Twankey's waist is simply a length of rope with items of clothing sewn in place.

As with any part of this production, if you or your pupils can think of a better way to design, make or paint props to use in the show – go for it. The whole idea of the pantomime is to exercise your class's imagination and to get everyone thinking and working together as a team.

Programme

A simple way to make your production more professional is to ask your pupils to design and write a programme to give away to members of the audience. This doesn't need to be any more complicated than a single sheet of paper, printed on both sides and folded in half. Most modern word processors will have a template to allow you to do just this.

The show programme should list the names of everyone involved in the production – from the cast list to those pupils who painted the scenery and made props and everyone in between. Of course, if you want to include my name as scriptwriter – I'll be eternally grateful!

On the front of the programme, add the date(s) the show will take place, the venue and the time. If you can, add colourful pictures or clip art to really make the programme something the audience will want to take home with them.

Programmes are great keepsakes for your pupils to remind them about the show after the big night has been and gone. Encourage everyone to sign their friends' programmes and keep them safely for the future. I've still got some of the programmes from plays I appeared in when I was at school.

Music

I've marked places in the *Aladdin* script where you can include songs and simple dance routines. There are also places where you can use incidental music as characters go on and off stage, or to provide an exciting atmosphere for a sword fight. If you decide to include music in your production, there are a couple of things you will need to bear in mind.

The first is that you will require a licence from the Performing Rights Society in order to stage your production, and this will be a different licence to the one you may have to use music in your day-to-day classroom activities. For more information, please visit:

www.mcps-prs-alliance.co.uk

If you want your characters to sing songs during the show, you also need to decide whether your pupils will sing live or mime to pre-recorded CDs. While it is obviously much better to have them sing live, it may be that their voices simply aren't strong enough to be heard. If this is the case, consider getting everyone to sing the lyrics together: a group of voices will cover any mistakes a solo singer may make.

If you decide that your pupils will sing live during the performance, you'll need to provide them with backing music. If you have a parent or member of staff with the ability to play the piano or guitar, you could ask them to fill this role – although please be aware that arranging music is a difficult and time-consuming process. It may be simpler to purchase backing tracks on CD to use throughout the show.

Backing tracks are recordings of songs without the lyrics (although some of them can come with backing vocals if you choose). These songs are recorded to sound as close to the original version of the song as possible so, when your performers sing over the music, the end result can be very professional indeed. The songs are frequently offered in a number of different musical keys, suitable for male or female singers.

There are plenty of companies that provide backing tracks in CD and MP3 format. Take a look at:

www.musicbackingtracks.co.uk

www.backingtracksonline.co.uk

www.backingtracks.co.uk

As with any of the websites listed in this book, I have no affiliation with the companies listed above, and do not receive any form of commission from them.

Once you have your tracks, you need to work out how to play them. Many schools have a sound system over which music can be played. If you have access to equipment like this, set it up so that the speakers stand at either side of your stage area and the actual music player is situated in one of the side wings.

Of course, many productions use microphones to ensure the actors are heard when saying their lines and especially when singing over a backing track. If your school has a microphone or two, consider setting them up on stands at the front of the performance area in order to pick up and amplify everything that is said on stage.

In an ideal world, everyone would have a small microphone clipped to their costume and attached to a pack which sends the signal through to a receiver connected to the sound system. These are known as radio microphones, and they eliminate the need to have stands at the front of the stage. However, equipment such as this is usually way beyond the budget of any standard school production.

If you really want to use radio microphones, try contacting your local music shop, sound equipment retailer or professional theatre company. They may be able to hire the microphones, receivers and mixing desk to you or – even better – sponsor your performance and provide the equipment in return for an advert in your show programme.

If they are willing to hire or lend professional sound equipment, ask if there is anyone free to come along and run the sound for you on the day of the show. Having someone there to set everything up and troubleshoot any problems will make life much simpler!

Once you have your songs ready, you may want to include other music in your show. You could play some tunes in the background as your audience arrives, use a particular song as an introduction or overture to the performance, and even add to the atmosphere on stage by adding sound effects and brief snippets of entrance or exit music (also called 'stings').

Sound effects and stings can be collected from a variety of sources, from professionally produced sound effect CDs to websites that provide free sounds in MP3 format. You may also wish to consider asking your pupils to design their own sound effects in advance, using the techniques explained in the 'Musical youth' chapter to record everything from crowd cheers to the whooshing of flying carpets.

When you have a handful of effects and stings, print off a copy of the script and use this exclusively as a sound script. Mark any of the sound cues you intend to use as clearly as possible (I always use a fluorescent highlighter pen to make sure they're visible) and – most importantly – check that this script can be read in what will be the dim light of the stage wings during the show. You don't want to suddenly realize that you can't see what you're supposed to be doing just as the audience are taking their seats!

If it is especially dark in the wings, use a desk lamp with a low wattage bulb. This light won't be visible to the audience, and will save you from playing Widow Twankey's entrance music just as Aladdin and Abanazer are about to clash swords!

Dancing

If you are using songs in your production, you may want your pupils to dance as well. It can be quite difficult for performers to sing and dance at the same time, so it may be wise just to have the townspeople or spirits perform the moves while the lead actors concentrate on getting their words right!

My advice for dance routines is to make them as simple as possible. Watching everyone on stage turn to the left and then back to the centre at the same time is much more effective than a complex sequence of steps where the entire cast are all dancing out of synch with each other. If any of your pupils attend stage classes at the weekend, they may be able to demonstrate a few simple dance moves that everyone can follow.

Be wary of any including any routine where your actors have to stamp their feet. If you're using stand microphones at the front of your stage, they'll pick up each thump and amplify it like a thunder clap, drowning out the music and singers in one fell swoop! If in doubt, stick to hand movements only.

Blocking

It's now time to break out your director's chair and start putting everyone through their paces – but even this stage of the production can be broken down into easily manageable sections. The first of these is called blocking.

Blocking is simply where you tell everyone where and when they come onto the stage, where they move when they're on there, and when they leave. Do not try to do anything else at this point; no emotion or emphasis on certain lines or words – this is very basic 'move from left to right' stuff.

A word of caution here: like dance routines, stage movements are far more effective when they are kept simple. Try to ensure your characters only move when they have a reason to do so. It is also a good idea to make your pupils aware of where the audience will be sitting. If they turn their backs on the front of the stage, the audience simply won't be able to hear or understand what they're saying, and could lose track of the story.

Work out where everyone will be moving in advance of this session and mark it down in a copy of the script. This will be your master blocking copy, and will prove very useful during rehearsals if anyone forgets where they should be at a specific point of the show. Ask everyone to write their moves, entrances and exits in their own copy of the script – and mark that script clearly with their name.

Practise the blocking until all your actors and dancers know where they should be going and when. It is worth spending a fair amount of time on this section as, if anything goes wrong during the performance itself, everyone will know exactly where to pick up the action in order to continue.

Rehearsals

Once the blocking is completed, it's time to add some layers onto your actors' performances. This is where you'll be fine-tuning the emotion in what they're saying, and placing emphasis on certain words of dialogue in order to carry your audience along with the story.

However, please don't lose sight of what this is: a school production of *Aladdin*. While I'm not saying that you shouldn't strive for this to be the best play your pupils have ever staged, the overzealous director/teacher is a well-known figure of comedy for a very good reason. Accept that you will not get Royal Shakespeare Company performances from a group of children, and you'll save yourself a lot of indigestion later on!

Be aware also that you may have a great deal more invested in this production than your pupils. To them, this may just be another class project they work on for a while at school, then forget when they go home. You, on the other hand, may spend night after night feverishly slaving over scripts and set designs. This doesn't mean that your pupils don't want the show to be a success; children just have the ability to leave a project at the classroom door better than any teacher I've ever known!

Rehearsals are monotonous, frequently boring and can feel very, very long – especially to someone who doesn't have a lot to do on stage and has to spend their time sitting and watching everyone around them get to act. Arrange frequent breaks in proceedings (every 20 minutes or so is ideal), and try not to dwell on the same few pages of the script over and over again. If a scene isn't working the way you want it to, leave it and come back to it another day when you have a fresh pair of eyes.

Practise the play from start to finish, stopping and starting where necessary. Some directors like to rehearse scenes out of order, but this only helps to confuse pupils and stop them from knowing with any clarity what comes next.

For the first few rehearsals, allow your pupils to carry their scripts with them, while insisting that they learn their lines in time for a specific date. They may find it scary trying to perform without the safety net of a script in their hands for the first few times but – the sooner they can do it – the sooner they'll feel confident in their own performances. If they occasionally get stuck, ask one of your pupils to sit beside the stage, following a copy of the script and prompting the actors as needed.

The closer you get to your performance, the more you'll add into your rehearsals. First of all, everyone will be concentrating solely on their lines and blocking, but you'll soon be able to add the songs and dances in, followed by the props and any scenery that needs to be moved. This, eventually, will result in the use of microphones (if you have them) and sound effects.

Unfortunately, the more your rehearsals progress, the more you'll come to accept a universal theatrical truth: every time you add something new, the show will fall apart. It will happen. The first time the actors have to actually sing and dance instead of skipping that part and moving onto the next section of dialogue, they'll immediately forget where they should be going and what they should be saying. As soon as you add props, your pupils will drop them, break them and leave them in the wings when they're needed on stage.

All your hard work will disintegrate – but don't worry. *This is what rehearsals are for!* Don't let it get you or your pupils down – all they need to do is practise some more. And that will lead them to the dress rehearsal . . . .

Dress rehearsal

I'm sorry to have to tell you that, if you thought things were bad whenever you introduced a new element to previous rehearsals – this is going to be the mother load of pain and suffering.

A dress rehearsal is where you bring everything together for the first time. The actors will be wearing their costumes, the microphones will be set up, the music will be playing – and it will be a disaster of epic proportions.

Don't worry – there is a saying in the theatre that if you have a bad dress rehearsal, you'll have a good first night. The most important thing is that everyone keeps going! If Twankey's laundry collapses around the actors – they must keep going! If every one of the spirits forgets the dance routine – keep going! If Abanazer runs on stage for the sword fight without being able to find his sword – keep going! (This actually happened to me when I was playing Abanazer in Northern Ireland. One of the other actors had moved my sword to put her costume down and, as I dashed off to collect it, I realized that I had no idea where it was! Thinking quickly, I grabbed something else to use as a weapon and I may be the only Abanazer ever to have fought Aladdin with the magic lamp itself!)

Explain to your pupils that they won't be able to stop during the actual performance and start again once any problems are sorted out (unless there's a major problem that would make continuing unsafe, of course), so they must do everything in their power to keep the action moving forward. If they have to invent new dialogue on the spot, move to where they shouldn't be or even take over another character's lines in order to keep the show running – that's what they must do. After all, while you and the cast know the script inside out, this will be the first time the audience will have seen the show and – nine times out of ten – they won't know anything was wrong until you tell them afterwards.

So, that's the dress rehearsal out of the way – now it's time for the big night . . .

The show

Whether you're staging a single performance or a whole week of pantomimes for the local community, the first night is a terrifying experience – so don't make it any more nerve-wracking than it needs to be! It's now too late to change anything, and fussing round the cast as they get into their costumes with suggestions of how the flying carpet chase could be improved will only add to the nerves and confuse people. This is the time to go wish everyone luck (or, in theatre terms, tell them to 'break a leg') then sit out with the rest of the audience and enjoy watching what your pupils can do.

You'll be amazed at how a few first-night nerves can really add to a performance. The fact that everyone is so desperate to get things right will help concentration and build the emotion on stage. Of course, things will go wrong but – so long as no one is in any danger of being hurt – just let it slide and trust your pupils to find a way out of it. They'll do just that and will probably surprise you with the ingenuity they use to keep things going.

After the show, it's time to relax and celebrate. If you have another performance the following day, don't give out any notes or suggestions for how problems could be solved – just let everyone bask in the glow of the applause they will have deservedly received. Oh, and you might want to have a few words planned for when the audience demands a speech from the show's director!

Pictures

If you do stage a production of the Aladdin script included in this book, I'd love to hear about it! Please email:

drama@tommydonbavand.com

You can use the same address if you want to ask me anything connected with the exercises in this book. I'll be putting a gallery of production photos online for you to share with other teachers around the country so, if you can send some pictures of your rehearsals or final show, all the better!

7 Aladdin script

You can either photocopy these pages for your production of *Aladdin* or download a text file of this script from the Continuum Books website:

www.continuumbooks.com/resources/9781855394469

You have permission to change any aspect of the script to suit your needs, however the reselling of the script is prohibited.

Aladdin

by Tommy Donbavand

www.tommydonbavand.com

Characters

ALADDIN – the hero

WISHEE WASHEE – his foolish brother

ABANAZER – the bad guy

SLAVE OF THE RING – a trapped spirit

WIDOW TWANKEY – an over-the-top dame

PRINCESS BLOSSOM – a beautiful girl

THE EMPEROR – Princess Blossom's father

CHOP and SUEY – bumbling policemen

GENIE – a powerful spirit

DAISY, ROSE, PANSY – handmaidens to the Princess

TOWNSPEOPLE, POLICEMEN, SPIRITS, DANCERS

VOICE – the voice of the Sphinx

LORD CHANCELLOR – the Lord Chancellor

ACT ONE

Scene 1
Exterior: Sphinx – Night

Lightning flashes, thunder rolls.

ABANAZER enters and stands before the monument, back to the audience, his arms flung high in the air.

ABANAZER
To those past lords of evil kind, I leave the righteous far behind. I hate the good, despise the weak. Bestow on me the power I seek!

Lightning flashes wildly. Abanazer spins around and faces the audience, his face lit eerily.

ABANAZER
At last, the elements are right! Only once a thousand years do the keepers of the night offer up their hidden secrets. Tonight I, Abanazer, the greatest wizard of all time, shall fulfil my quest for power, and take over the world!

He laughs maniacally. Lightning flashes again.

A voice echoes out.

VOICE
Who dares disturb the sleep of those long dead?

Abanazer spins around to face the Sphinx, and drops to his knees.

ABANAZER
It is I, my lord. Abanazer, your humble servant.

VOICE
You desire to control the darkest of powers?

ABANAZER
I do my lord. I shall rule the world in your servitude. Show me the source of this power, and the lords of darkness shall be worshipped once more.

VOICE
Very well! Listen carefully Abanazer . . .

ABANAZER
Yes, my lord.

VOICE
There is a cave in China – the Cave of Wonders. Hidden within it lies a lamp.

ABANAZER
A lamp? But I . . .

VOICE
Do not question my words!

Abanazer cowers before the Sphinx.

VOICE	The lamp is the source of the power you seek. Obtain this lamp, and you shall have your reward. But only one may enter the cave, Abanazer. A boy. Enter the cave yourself, and you shall spend eternity in the fires of the underworld!

Lightning flashes and thunder rolls again. The storm subsides.

Abanazer gets to his feet and moves downstage.

ABANAZER	So, it is a lamp I seek, hidden deep within a cave in China. But who is this one who can enter the cave? I must summon the Slave of my magic ring.

He waves his hand over the ring. The SLAVE OF THE RING enters, wearing an apron, and holding a feather duster.

SLAVE	Oh, it's you. Typical, I was just in the middle of dusting my 40-piece Royal Doulton service.
ABANAZER	How dare you address me in that manner?! I am your lord and master.
SLAVE	Ooh, touchy.
	(*in monotone*) You have summoned the Slave of the magic ring, oh all empowering master. I am yours to command, and shall obey.
	(*happy again*) Now, what can I do you for?
ABANAZER	There is a cave in China. The Cave of Wonders . . .
SLAVE	China? Ooh, I could murder a sweet and sour pork.
ABANAZER	Silence! I seek the lamp that lies within the cave.
SLAVE	What, that rusty old thing? I shouldn't bother if I were you, it's the devil to keep clean.

Abanazer glares at the Slave.

ABANAZER	One more remark like that, and you'll have a 400-piece Royal Doulton service – little sharp pieces.

The Slave looks hurt.

ABANAZER	Do you know where this Cave of Wonders lies?
SLAVE	(sulking) Might do . . .
ABANAZER	Tell me!

SLAVE	Oh, don't shout! I've had a terrible morning. My little dog's not well.
	He reacts to the cries of 'awww!' from the audience, hamming it up.
SLAVE	I had to take him to the vets. The vet said he had to put him down.
ABANAZER	Why?
SLAVE	Because he was too heavy. Poor little thing. He hasn't got any legs.
ABANAZER	Hasn't got any legs? What do you call him?
SLAVE	It didn't matter, he never comes running.
ABANAZER	What's his *name*?
SLAVE	Oh, I call him Handyman.
ABANAZER	Why?
SLAVE	Because he does little jobs all over the house! The vet said he has to wear a muzzle when he goes out.
ABANAZER	A muzzle? Is he mad?
SLAVE	Well, he's not exactly pleased about it.
ABANAZER	Will you shut up! If there's one thing I hate, it's dogs. In fact, the only things I hate more than dogs are children. Snivelling, snotty, smelly children!
	He glares out into the audience.
ABANAZER	There aren't any children here today, are there?
	Audience cries 'Yes!'
ABANAZER	Well if there are, they'd better hide themselves from me. I'm not in a very nice mood.
SLAVE	In which case, I'm not telling you where the Cave of Wonders is!
	The Slave winks at the audience. Abanazer tries to control his rage.
ABANAZER	(*struggles to sound nice*) OK, I'm asking nicely. Would you . . . *please* . . . tell me dear Slave – where is the Cave of Wonders?
SLAVE	That's better. Forty leagues west of Old Pekin, through the enchanted forest, and second star to the right.

ABANAZER	There, that wasn't so hard, was it? And who is this one who alone can enter the cave?
SLAVE	Who?
ABANAZER	This boy who can fetch me the lamp – who is he?
SLAVE	Oh, that one's easy! That's Aladdin!
	MUSIC: MYSTICAL CHORDS

_____

Scene 2
Exterior: Marketplace – Day

Townspeople and market traders go about their business. They bring on stage everything needed for this scene, including props, drapes and the sign for Twankey's Laundry.

Suddenly, a whistle blows from off stage. ALADDIN, clutching a handful of stolen flowers, is chased onto the stage and across the stage by CHOP and SUEY, the Chinese policemen.

He sings as he's being chased, steals items from the market stalls, and narrowly misses being caught several times.

MUSIC: OPENING SONG

He snatches an apple from a stall. The market traders join the chase.

Abanazer enters and watches the chase with interest.

Aladdin temporarily loses his pursuers. He grins at the audience as the music continues.

ALADDIN	Alright gang! Oh, come on – let's hear it! My name's Aladdin, and when I shout 'Alright gang', I want you all to shout back 'Alright Al'! Can you do that?

The audience shout 'yes'.

ALADDIN	Alright gang!

The kids shout 'Alright Al'!

Chop and Suey rush back on to the stage, followed by the market traders.

SUEY	There he is Sarge!
ALADDIN	Oops! Gotta run gang! Catch you later!

The chase resumes!

Aladdin leaps off the stage, runs through the audience, and out of the auditorium (if possible).

Chop and Suey reach the edge of the stage out of breath, and watch him go angrily. The market traders gather behind them, shaking their fists.

CHOP	I'll get you for this Aladdin!
SUEY	We'll have to catch him first, Sarge!

Chop slaps Suey across the head, and they leave. The market traders go back to their stalls.

Abanazer steps forward, smiling.

ABANAZER   So, this is Aladdin? The boy who can enter the cave and get me the lamp. A cunning little fox, so I shall have to be even more cunning to win his trust. I need to find a simpleton who can lead me to him.

WISHEE WASHEE enters, and starts asking the townspeople if they've seen Aladdin.

WISHEE   Have you seen Aladdin? My mum's been looking for him. I need to find him (etc.).

Abanazer smiles wickedly at the audience.

ABANAZER   Don't you just love it when a plan comes together?

He sweeps to the back of the stage to keep an eye on Wishee Washee.

The townspeople gesture Wishee Washee towards the audience.

WISHEE   Wotcha kids!

He waves to the audience.

WISHEE   Oh, you can do better than that. But I suppose we haven't been introduced properly. My name is Wishee Washee, and I need to know yours – so shout it out after three. One, two three . . .

The kids shout their names.

WISHEE   No, you'll need to shout louder than that, I haven't got my glasses on. One, two, three . . .

The kids shout again.

WISHEE	That's better. Now whenever I shout 'Wotcha kids!' you can all shout back 'Wotcha Wishee!'. Shall we have a go? Wotcha kids!
	The kids shout 'Wotcha Wishee!'
WISHEE	Louder than that. Wotcha kids!
	'Wotcha Wishee!' louder still!
WISHEE	That's great. Now, the townspeople said you'd seen my brother Aladdin. Have you seen him? You have? Was he in trouble again? Oh dear – my mum won't be happy. What had he stolen this time?
	The kids shout 'flowers'.
WISHEE	Flowers?
	A voice off stage left startles him.
TWANKEY	Well, I hope they were for his mum!
	MUSIC: TWANKEY'S ENTRANCE
	WIDOW TWANKEY sweeps onto the stage carrying a large shopping basket.
	She spots the audience.
TWANKEY	Oh, hello. It's me, Widow Twankey – owner of the town laundry, local superstar and the biggest sex symbol around these parts since Girls Aloud dropped by for a panda curry! Hello, Wishee, love. How are you?
WISHEE	I'm fine mum, but I'm not sure about Aladdin.
TWANKEY	Did I hear you say he'd bought me some flowers?
WISHEE	Well, not *bought*, exactly . . .
TWANKEY	Oh no, I can't be doing with him in trouble again. I've got enough on my plate with all the washing for the Emperor's birthday party tomorrow. Now, you go off and see if you can find him.
WISHEE	OK, mum.
	Wishee exits. Twankey watches him go.
TWANKEY	Nice boy, but about as sharp as a sack of wet mice.
	She removes one of her shoes, and rubs her foot.

Making a Drama out of a Crisis   *Aladdin* script

TWANKEY	Ooh, that's better. I've shopped for China today! I've had to buy all sorts of linen ready for the Emperor's party.
	She digs into her shopping basket and pulls out bags of chocolate buttons.
TWANKEY	But I did buy a whole basketful of these. Who wants some, then? Shout out, that's it.
	The kids try to catch the thrown offerings.
TWANKEY	Oh, it's been such a day.
	MUSIC: TWANKEY'S SONG
	Twankey takes elaborate bows. When she's done, she turns to see Abanazer applauding politely from the side of the stage.
TWANKEY	Ooh, look. It's George Clooney's dad.
	She swaggers over.
TWANKEY	I take it then, that you enjoyed my performance?
ABANAZER	It was sublime. Your voice is like angel's tears dripping down onto fine crystal.
	Twankey is thrilled.
TWANKEY	Ooh, do you really think so?
ABANAZER	I do indeed. It is rare to hear such melancholy melodies from a mystifying mellifluous maiden.
TWANKEY	Who's swallowed a dictionary then? They normally say barbarous belching from a blobby blancmange.
ABANAZER	Oh, how could anyone not adore such beauty.
TWANKEY	Ooh, well I have been working out. Every morning it's up for ten, down for ten – and then the other sock . . .
ABANAZER	And such a figure . . .
TWANKEY	I've taken up jogging to keep my weight down.
ABANAZER	Has it worked?
TWANKEY	Oh yes – it's down around my bum now!
ABANAZER	But, enough of this idle banter. It has been so long since we last met.
TWANKEY	We've met? I think I would have remembered you.
ABANAZER	Alas, not since your wedding day. I am the brother of your late husband.

TWANKEY	My Cedric had a brother?

Abanazer bows deeply.

ABANAZER	Abanazer Twankey, at your service.
TWANKEY	I don't remember you at the wedding. Mind you, I don't remember much about the wedding at all, except arriving at the church and seeing the aisle stretched out before me, then looking up and seeing the altar, and then hearing the congregation singing a hymn. That's exactly what I thought when I saw Cedric standing there all expectant – I'll alter him!
ABANAZER	Alas, many years and many adventures have taken their toll. I am no longer the dashing hero that once I was.
TWANKEY	Our Cedric was only ever dashing when he was disappearing with my purse down the off-licence.

Wishee and Aladdin enter. Aladdin still carries the cheap handful of flowers.

WISHEE	I found him, mum.

Twankey grabs Aladdin by the ear.

TWANKEY	Now then, lad. What have you been up to this time?
ALADDIN	Nothing mum. Honest.

Twankey lifts him higher.

ALADDIN	Alright, alright. I needed some flowers. They're for the girl of my dreams.
ABANAZER	The girl of your dreams? She must be special.

Aladdin and Wishee notice Abanazer for the first time.

ALADDIN	Who are you?
TWANKEY	Boys, say hello to your uncle Abanazer.
ALADDIN	I didn't know we had an uncle. You always said my dad was an only child.
TWANKEY	No, I said he should have been an only child – his parents used to send him to school with his sandwiches wrapped in a road map, and then move before he came home.
ABANAZER	Your father was a handsome man.
TWANKEY	Are you sure we're talking about the same Cedric?

ALADDIN	Yeah, didn't you always say he had something wrong with his legs?
WISHEE	Yes. They wouldn't walk past pubs.

Twankey slaps Wishee.

ABANAZER	But, this isn't getting flowers for the girl of your dreams, young Aladdin, my boy.

He pulls out a handful of gold coins. The others look on amazed. He hands a coin to Aladdin.

ABANAZER	This should buy your sweetheart a wonderful bouquet.
ALADDIN	Wow! Thanks uncle.

Aladdin exits, clutching the coin.

TWANKEY	Wishee, follow him. Make sure he doesn't get into more trouble.
WISHEE	But mum, I want to stay here and tell uncle Abanazer about the girl of my dreams.

Twankey raises her hand again.

TWANKEY	Wishee . . .
WISHEE	Alright, I'm going.

He follows Aladdin off.

Twankey links arms with Abanazer.

TWANKEY	Why don't you come and have a look around my laundry, brother-in-law, dear?

She winks at the audience, and leads Abanazer away.

_____

Scene 3
Exterior: Palace – Day

Aladdin enters, clutching a beautiful bouquet of flowers.

ALADDIN   Alright, gang! Hey, I've got my flowers – now I've just got to find the courage to give them to the girl of my dreams.

He smiles to himself.

ALADDIN   Oh, she's beautiful. She's got these big, brown eyes, and this long hair, and . . .

WISHEE   There you are!

ALADDIN   Oh, hello, Wishee.

WISHEE   I've followed you halfway across Pekin. Wotcha kids! What are you doing here?

ALADDIN   I've come to give these flowers to the girl of my dreams. In fact, I'll let you into a secret – I'm thinking of asking her to marry me.

WISHEE   But, this is the Emperor's palace. We'll be thrown in jail if we're caught hanging around here.

ALADDIN   Well, she, er . . . works here . . .

WISHEE   Oh, I see. Well, what's her name? What does she look like?

Aladdin takes a crumpled envelope from his pocket and hands it over to Wishee. He examines it.

WISHEE   You're in love with a gas bill?

ALADDIN   No, not the bill! The stamp!

WISHEE   The stamp? But that's a picture of the Princess. You know why they put a picture of her face on the stamp, don't you?

Aladdin shakes his head.

WISHEE   Because if they put her bum on there, no one would lick it.

Aladdin snatches the envelope back.

WISHEE   But, what has the Princess got to do with the girl of your . . . Oh, no! Aladdin, tell me I'm not right! Tell me the girl of your dreams isn't Princess Blossom!

Aladdin blushes and hides his face in the flowers.

WISHEE	But she's a Princess, and you're the lowly son of a washerwoman! You couldn't ever be together.
ALADDIN	I'll leave that for her to decide, thank you.
WISHEE	But, Aladdin, the Emperor has decreed that anyone who looks upon the Princess's face shall be executed. She's not worth losing your head over.
ALADDIN	I've already lost my heart to her. My head might as well be next.
WISHEE	How long as this been going on?
ALADDIN	Two weeks. Two glorious weeks. I'm telling you Wishee, as soon as she meets me, she'll feel the same way.
WISHEE	You're going to ask her to marry you, and you've never even met her?
ALADDIN	No, do you think I'm stupid? I'm not going to stride right up to her and declare my love – I'm a commoner. No, I've been staring at her in her bedroom from a branch in the great oak tree, or hiding in the bushes, and watching her stroll through the gardens.
WISHEE	Oh, well, that's much better. She'll be much happier to meet you once she finds out you've been stalking her for a fortnight!
ALADDIN	But, today is different. I'm going to climb over the palace walls, find her, introduce the flowers, and give her myself . . . er, I mean give her the flowers, and introduce myself.

He starts to exit, Wishee catches him.

WISHEE	But, what about the guards?
ALADDIN	I didn't bring enough flowers for them.

He strides off. Wishee chases after him.

Scene 4
Interior: Palace Gardens – Day

PRINCESS BLOSSOM sits with her three ladies-in-waiting, ROSE, DAISY and PANSY, discussing the Emperor's impending birthday celebrations.

ROSE   . . . and we could have trapeze acts, and jugglers . . .

DAISY   Tumblers! I love tumblers!

PANSY   I'd love to see a strongman act. They could get together and decide which one would lift me over his head, and carry me away.

They all giggle behind their fans. The Princess sighs.

BLOSSOM   I'd like to go outside the palace for the day. To see the marketplace, to meet the people.

The ladies-in-waiting are shocked.

ROSE   But Princess, you've never been outside the palace walls in your life.

BLOSSOM   I know . . .

DAISY   It's very rough . . .

PANSY   You wouldn't like it out there. One time when I was in the marketplace, this man followed me all the way home. Or at least he would have done if he hadn't managed to get his bus pass back.

BLOSSOM   I'd just like the chance to find out for myself. I feel so trapped in here, never seeing anything of the world. I wish someone would arrive who could just take me away from all of this.

ALADDIN (*O.S.*)   Hello . . .

Blossom and her ladies-in-waiting spin around to see Aladdin standing behind them, nervously holding his flowers.

ROSE   A burglar!

DAISY   A murderer!

PANSY   A cutie-pie!

BLOSSOM   Who are you?

Aladdin summons the courage to speak.

ALADDIN	I live in the city, Your Majesty. I came here to see you.
ROSE	Shall I fetch the palace guards, Majesty?
BLOSSOM	No. I don't think he'll do much harm with those flowers.

Aladdin holds the flowers out to her.

ALADDIN	They're for you.

Blossom shyly takes her flowers, and turns to her ladies.

BLOSSOM	Leave us.
DAISY	Your Majesty?
BLOSSOM	I said leave us.
PANSY	I think I should stay, to keep an eye on him . . .
BLOSSOM	Now!

The ladies-in-waiting all bow, and exit, whispering to each other.

BLOSSOM	Are those really for me?
ALADDIN	Yeah – they're a present.

He hands over the flowers.

BLOSSOM	Thank you, they're beautiful.
ALADDIN	Yes, you are . . . I mean, they are.

Blossom sits.

BLOSSOM	Why don't you come and sit down, and we'll talk. It's a lot more comfortable than the great oak tree.
ALADDIN	OK, but . . . You saw me?!
BLOSSOM	Every night for two weeks . . .
ALADDIN	Oh, I . . . er . . .
BLOSSOM	It's OK. I was hoping for a chance to speak to you, and ask your name.
ALADDIN	You did? Well, my name's Aladdin!
BLOSSOM	Aladdin. I don't think I've heard that name before. Are you from Pekin?
ALADDIN	No, my family come from far away. We're rich, and we live in a castle, and . . . Oh, what's the use? I'm the son of a poor washerwoman.

He drops his head.

BLOSSOM	That's nothing to be ashamed of. It must be wonderful to be able to roam the marketplace.
ALADDIN	And never have the money to buy anything. I think it would great to be rich, and live in a palace.
BLOSSOM	And have people tell you what to do, and when to do it. But, just to be able to climb the great oak whenever you wanted . . .
ALADDIN	You've never climbed the great oak?
BLOSSOM	I've never climbed any tree. I was never allowed.

Aladdin stands, and holds out his hand.

ALADDIN	Then it's time you learned.

The Princess glances around.

BLOSSOM	Now?
ALADDIN	Why not? There's no time like the present.

He helps Blossom to her feet, and they stare into each other's eyes silently for a moment.

ALADDIN	Princess, I have to ask you a question.
BLOSSOM	Yes?
ALADDIN	Do you believe in . . . in . . .
BLOSSOM	UFOs?
ALADDIN	No . . .
BLOSSOM	The Loch Ness Monster?
ALADDIN	No.
BLOSSOM	Love at first sight?
ALADDIN	Yes, that's it. Love at first sight . . .

They make as if to kiss, when a shout disturbs them.

EMPEROR (O.S.)	Search the grounds, they're here somewhere!

Blossom spins around.

BLOSSOM	Father!

Aladdin turns her to face him.

ALADDIN	I have to ask you another question.
BLOSSOM	Quickly!
ALADDIN	Do you think that a guy like you, and a girl like me could ever be married?

BLOSSOM	Oh, Aladdin – I wish it could be. You're the only person who's ever climbed a tree for me! But my father is arranging my wedding. I have to marry a prince.
EMPEROR (*O.S.*)	Here they are!

The EMPEROR enters, followed by Chop and Suey, and the ladies-in-waiting.

EMPEROR	A commoner? In the palace gardens?! And he's talking to the Princess! Guards, seize him!

Chop and Suey grab Aladdin's arms, and throw him to the ground.

BLOSSOM	Father, no!
EMPEROR	It's alright, my daughter. He'll be out of your sight soon enough.

He stands over Aladdin.

EMPEROR	Do you know the penalty for gazing upon the face of the Princess?

Suey makes a beheading action.

EMPEROR	That's right. And I'll see that your sentence is carried out immediately.
BLOSSOM	No!
ALADDIN	But, Your Majesty, you don't understand. I'm here for your birthday celebrations.
EMPEROR	What?
ALADDIN	I'm part of the entertainment. I came in to measure the size of the stage, and accidentally wandered into the gardens.

The Emperor ponders this for a moment. He snaps his fingers, and Chop releases his grip on Aladdin.

EMPEROR	You're here for my party?

Aladdin stands and nods.

EMPEROR	I'm having a party?

Aladdin nods faster.

BLOSSOM	It was supposed to be a surprise, father.
EMPEROR	Oh, never mind that!

He puts his arm around Aladdin's shoulder, and leads him inside the palace.

EMPEROR So, my boy, what do you do? A conjurer? I love magic tricks, or perhaps you're a singer? I shall be needing somebody to sing 'Happy Birthday' to me . . .

He leads Aladdin away. Princess Blossom picks up her flowers, glares at her ladies-in-waiting, and follows.

MUSIC: POLICE MUSIC

———————————————

Scene 5
Ext. City Street – Day

Chop and Suey are patrolling the street, searching for bad guys.

CHOP	Right, PC Suey, it is our duty to patrol this area, and make sure that no troublemakers try to force their way inside the palace.
SUEY	Right O.
CHOP	We have to keep the peace, and make sure that everyone at the Emperor's birthday party behaves in an orderly fashion.
SUEY	Right O.
CHOP	And, if anyone does get out of line, it is our job to take control of the situation, and detain the troublemakers.
SUEY	Right O.
CHOP	Why do you keep saying Right O?
SUEY	Because you're standing on my right toe!

Chop moves away, angrily.

SUEY	Ooh! I'm really excited about this party, aren't you Sarge?
CHOP	PC Suey – we are not attending this party for reasons of fun, we will be there to make sure that everything runs as smoothly as possible.

Suey looks disappointed.

CHOP	And . . . I shall be singing.
SUEY	Y' what? You? Singing?
CHOP	I have a very good voice, I'll have you know. I have sung before the Duke of York, the Prince Of Wales . . .
SUEY	And about a dozen other local pubs!
CHOP	Well, haven't you ever wanted to be anything other than a policeman?
SUEY	Oh yeah, I got a job as a postman once, but every day when I got into work, they gave me the sack!

He laughs at his own joke.

SUEY	They gave me the sack! Oh, never mind.

Making a Drama out of a Crisis   *Aladdin* **script**

CHOP	Well, I've sung with the greats. Frank Sinatra, Elvis Presley, Harry Connick Jr.
SUEY	Yeah, they were on the radio while you were in the bath!
	Chop turns away in a huff.
SUEY	Why don't you practise your singing now, Sarge?
CHOP	Now? We're on duty.
SUEY	There's no one else about, and you'll need all the practice you can get if you're going to sing for the Emperor. I could be your musical director.
CHOP	I could do with having a rehearsal, but you don't know which key I sing in.
SUEY	Is it Yale?
CHOP	Could I have an A flat, please?
SUEY	Just give him an A, he'll flatten it himself.
	MUSIC: CHOP and SUEY'S SONG
SUEY	That was terrible!
	Chop chases him off, blowing his own whistle.

Scene 6
Interior: Twankey's Laundry – Day

Wishee Washee stumbles in carrying a huge pile of washing. He stumbles around the stage, almost dropping it on the audience.

WISHEE   Mum? Mum! Where are you? I've got the next lot of clothes to wash.

TWANKEY (*O.S.*)   I'm outside, putting the clean washing on the line.

WISHEE   Oh. Hang on, we haven't got a washing line!

TWANKEY   We have now!

Twankey spins on, uncurling a washing line from around herself. It stretches from one side of the stage to the other. Twankey runs around the back, and comes on again. This time, the line reaches halfway across.

WISHEE   That's a weird way to dry the washing . . .

TWANKEY   Well, I've got so much to do, I've got a little behind.

WISHEE   Oh, I wouldn't say that.

TWANKEY   You watch what you're saying! I'll stop your pocket money!

WISHEE   You don't give me any pocket money . . .

TWANKEY   Well, I'll start, then stop it.

They start to pull items of underwear out of the washer, and roll them through the mangle.

WISHEE   How come we're not rich, mum?

TWANKEY   I don't know Wishee, love. I keep doing the lottery, and the pools. Mind you, we nearly won this week.

WISHEE   Did we?

TWANKEY   Yes, my homes were alright, my aways were alright – but my draws let me down.

She pulls an old pair of bloomers out of the washer.

WISHEE   Well, couldn't you marry someone who's rich?

TWANKEY   Ooh, Wishee. If I had a pound for every rich gentleman who's proposed to me . . .

WISHEE   What would you do?

TWANKEY	Buy a packet of polos. Now come on, let's get this washing finished.
WISHEE	We can't – the washer's bunged up.
TWANKEY	Then go and get the unbunger!

Wishee reaches off into the wings and grabs a large brush on a huge pole. He waves it over the heads of the audience, causing them to duck.

WISHEE	Ooh, sorry . . . watch it . . . careful . . .

He manages to get the end of the brush into the washer, and starts to unbung it.

MUSIC: POLICE MUSIC

Chop and Suey enter.

CHOP	'Ello, 'ello, 'ello! Is this the right address, Constable?

Suey gets out a sheet of paper.

SUEY	I think so, Sarge. 999 Letsbe Avenue.
CHOP	You idiot, that's the address of the police station!
SUEY	Oh, sorry . . .

He turns the paper over.

SUEY	The Street Of A Thousand Chopsticks, No. 47, with a portion of fried rice.
TWANKEY	Can I help you, officers? Ooh, I do like a man in uniform . . .!
CHOP	We are here on behalf of the Emperor, to make sure that all the laundry will be done in time for his party tomorrow.
WISHEE	Well, it would be, except our washer's bunged up.
SUEY	Bunged up? Let's have a look . . .

Suey leans over the edge of the washer and peers in. Wishee swings the unbunger around, and knocks him in.

WISHEE	Ooh, 'eck! He's fallen in.
CHOP	Out of the way, I'll get him.

Chop leans over the edge of the washer, and gets a bucket of water in the face.

CHOP	Look at me! My uniform's soaked.
TWANKEY	That's no problem – we'll just wring you out.

Twankey grabs hold of Chop, and pushes him into the mangle. She turns the handle, and rolls him through.

TWANKEY	Ooh, he's a tough one. Give me a hand, Wishee.
WISHEE	OK, mum.

They roll Chop through the mangle, and pick up a life-size cardboard cut-out of him from the other side.

WISHEE	Ooh, 'eck! It's the thin blue line!
TWANKEY	What about his mate . . .!

They rush over to the washer, and pull out a smaller child dressed in a policeman's uniform. He jumps up and down angrily.

TWANKEY	Ooh, look. He's got turn-ups in his underpants.

The tiny Suey grabs the cardboard cut-out of Chop and runs off stage angrily.

Aladdin passes them on his way in.

ALADDIN	Hiya mum, hiya Wishee. Alright gang!

(Alright, Al!)

ALADDIN	What happened to Chop and Suey?
TWANKEY	They fell into a vat of Slimfast. Now come on you two, we have to get this washing finished in time for the Emperor's birthday party.
ALADDIN	Oh no, you don't.
TWANKEY	Oh yes, we do.

Aladdin gets the audience to join in.

ALADDIN	Oh no, you don't.
TWANKEY	Oh yes, we do.
ALADDIN	Oh no, you don't.

Twankey turns to the audience.

TWANKEY	How do you lot know? Have you read the script? What are you talking about lad?

ALADDIN	We don't need to do the washing, 'cos we're all going to the party!
WISHEE	We're going to a party at the palace?
TWANKEY	Oh, I always knew it would happen! I can just see myself mingling with the crème de la menthe of society.
ALADDIN	Well . . . we're not exactly guests – we're performing for the Emperor.
WISHEE	Who is?
ALADDIN	You, and me, and mum, and uncle Abanazer. I have to get inside the palace, and talk to the Princess again.
TWANKEY	Even better, I can wow them all with my wonderful singing voice. I got a sitting ovation in Vienna once, you know. It would have been better, except they were still booing the bloke before me while I was on.

She starts to rummage through piles of clothing.

TWANKEY	Now, what shall I wear. My Gucci? My Versace? My Mitsubishi?

Aladdin pulls a tiny tutu out from one of the piles.

ALADDIN	Actually mum, you're better wearing this – I told them we were ballerinas!
TWANKEY	What?!
ALADDIN	It's the first thing that came into my head!

Twankey grabs the unbunger, and starts chasing Aladdin around the laundry. Wishee chases after her, trying to get to her to stop.

MUSIC: CHASE MUSIC

─────────────────────────────

Scene 7
Exterior: Palace – Day

Abanazer enters to hisses and boos!

ABANAZER   You can boo all you like, I don't care. My plan is coming together nicely. I have won the trust of Aladdin and his freakish family – he's so desperate to get inside the palace and talk to the Princess, he'll do anything I ask in return. He will get me the lamp.

He grins at the audience.

ABANAZER   You know, sometimes, I amaze even myself . . . But, I need to make sure the rest of his inbred clan behave as they should, and for that, I'll need a little assistance.

He rubs his magic ring. The Slave of the Ring enters, wearing a dressing gown and a shower cap, and carrying a loofah.

SLAVE   Oh, it's you. Can we make this quick? I've got a bath running . . .

ABANAZER   One day I will teach you not to talk to me in such a disrespectful tone!

SLAVE   And I could teach you how to knit.

ABANAZER   Silence! I need a way to keep Aladdin's idiot family from spoiling my plan. I must get the lamp.

SLAVE   Look no further. I think your answer's heading this way.

Chop and Suey enter. Suey's police uniform is a little too small still.

SUEY   How are you feeling now Sarge?

CHOP   A bit deflated still. We need to keep an eye on that family, Constable – they're trouble.

ABANAZER   Perfect! With these two fools under my control, I cannot fail.

He approaches Chop and Suey.

CHOP   Halt! Who goes there?

ABANAZER   Chief Inspector Abanazer. Your new superior officer.

CHOP	Chief Inspector Abanazer? I've not heard of any new chief inspector. Have you, Constable?
	Suey pushes past Chop.
SUEY	I'll handle this, Sarge. Now then you – what if we don't believe that you're our new chief inspector?
ABANAZER	Then I'll pull your legs off, and throw them over there . . .
SUEY	Oooh!
ABANAZER	I'll pull your arms off, and throw them over there . . .
SUEY	Oooh!
ABANAZER	Then I'll rip your head off, and throw it over there . . .
SUEY	Ooooh!
ABANAZER	What do you say to that?
SUEY	That sounds like me all over!
	Suey darts back, and hides behind Chop.
ABANAZER	Supposing I was to arrest you for GBH.?
SUEY	What, Grievous Boldily Harm?
ABANAZER	No, Getting Behind Him!
CHOP	Hang on, if you're our new chief inspector, how come you're not wearing a uniform.
ABANAZER	Because I'm undercover.
	Chop points to the Slave.
CHOP	What about him?
ABANAZER	He's underwater.
SLAVE	Have we quite finished here? My rubber duck will be getting lonely.
ABANAZER	Then do as I command, and put them under my control.
SLAVE	Your wish is my command, oh master.
	The Slave waves his loofah in the air. Chop and Suey's eyes become glazed, and they stand rigid.
SLAVE	Done. Can I go now?
ABANAZER	Yes, yes, get away with you.
SLAVE	There's no need to be rude!
	The Slave exits.

Making a Drama out of a Crisis   *Aladdin* script

	Abanazer waves his hand in front of Chop and Suey. They sway from side to side following it.
ABANAZER	You are both now completely under my control.
	Chop and Suey speak in monotone voices.
CHOP and SUEY	Yes, Chief Inspector.
ABANAZER	And you will help in my plan to have Aladdin fetch me the lamp?
CHOP and SUEY	Yes, Chief Inspector.
	Abanazer sneers at the audience.
ABANAZER	Sometimes, I'm so good, it scares me.
	With an evil laugh, he strides off stage, followed by a stumbling Chop and Suey.

_____

Scene 8
Interior: Palace – Day

The members of the royal court are all wearing party hats. The Emperor and Princess sit on thrones, watching the entertainment.

Chop and Suey stand at the rear of the room, watching for trouble.

The DANCERS perform a routine to the delight of the party guests. At the end, the Emperor applauds loudly, having a great time.

The LORD CHANCELLOR stands to announce the next act.

CHANCELLOR   Your Royal Highnesses, honoured guests, it is now my great honour to introduce our next act – all the way from the ancient theatres of Russia – The Bolshy Ballet.

MUSIC: SWAN LAKE

Wishee Washee, dressed in a tutu, ballet dances on, carrying a large, round balloon.

Abanazer follows, also dressed in a tutu, and also carrying a large, round balloon.

Aladdin is next, dressed the same, and with his balloon.

Widow Twankey finally dances on, dressed outrageously as a prima ballerina, and carrying a long thin balloon.

Aladdin nudges her, and she lets the balloon fly out into the audience. One of the party guests gives her a round balloon.

The routine begins with Wishee and Abanazer bouncing their balloons off each other's chests, and then curtseying to each other.

Aladdin follows suit, but Twankey hits her balloon hard into Aladdin's face, and he falls to the ground.

The routine continues: Wishee and Abanazer perform some skill with their balloons (rolling one between them, going under each other's legs, etc.) – and each time Aladdin and Twankey try to follow, Twankey messes it up, and Aladdin gets floored.

Eventually, Wishee, Abanazer and Twankey pirouette away, holding their arms out to catch Aladdin.

He resists for a moment, then runs and leaps into their arms. The momentum carries them over to the Princess's throne.

Aladdin kisses her.

The room is shocked. The Emperor jumps to his feet.

EMPEROR	Guards! Guards! Arrest that ballerina. He kissed the Princess!
BLOSSOM	Father, no!
EMPEROR	You mustn't worry yourself about him, my dear. He's a scoundrel, and he shall be punished.

Chop and Suey grab Aladdin, and force him to kneel before the Emperor.

EMPEROR	I let you off when you gazed upon my daughter's face in the palace gardens, young rascal – but now you've gone too far! Do you know the penalty for kissing the Princess?

Aladdin shakes his head.

EMPEROR	The penalty is death.

Twankey looks as though she may faint. Abanazer smiles.

BLOSSOM	But father, I kissed him back!
EMPEROR	You're in shock, my dear, but don't worry, it will all soon be over.
ALADDIN	I kissed the Princess because I'm in love with her! I'll come back some day and marry you Princess Blossom.
EMPEROR	That's not very likely . . .

He barks at Chop and Suey.

EMPEROR	Take him away and execute him!
CHOP and SUEY	Yes, Your Majesty.

Chop and Suey drag Aladdin to his feet. He takes one last look at the sobbing Princess and Widow Twankey, and allows himself to be led away.

Abanazer stops Chop and Suey just as they are about to leave.

ABANAZER   Do not execute Aladdin. Instead, take him to the old ravine outside the city at midnight. I'll meet you there.

CHOP and SUEY   Yes, Chief Inspector.

They drag Aladdin away as chaos continues to reign in the palace. The Emperor tries to comfort the Princess, and Wishee tries to console Widow Twankey.

Abanazer takes one last look at the trouble he has caused and, with an evil laugh, he sweeps out of the room.

MUSIC: DRAMATIC CHORDS

———————————————

Scene 9
Exterior: Ravine – Night

Lightning flashes across the sky. Abanazer stands in the wind.

ABANAZER   Now is the hour! The boy shall retrieve the lamp, and the power to take over the world shall be mine!

Chop and Suey drag Aladdin onto the stage.

ABANAZER   About time! You two get back to town, and put the word out that Aladdin's execution was swift, and painful.

CHOP and SUEY   Yes, Chief Inspector.

Chop and Suey exit.

ALADDIN   What are we doing here, uncle? And why did those policemen call you Chief Inspector?

ABANAZER   All shall be revealed in time, Aladdin, my boy – but first, I think a little gratitude is in order. I saved your measly neck from the executioner's blade.

ALADDIN   Yes, of course – thank you, uncle. But why do you want people to think I'm dead?

ABANAZER   Why then the Emperor won't send out any more of his legions to hunt you down . . .

Aladdin isn't convinced.

ALADDIN   Oh . . . OK.

ABANAZER   And, since I went to the trouble of saving your life – there is one little thing that you could do for me in return . . .

ALADDIN   Sure, uncle. What is it?

Abanazer looks around, as though someone might hear – then he steps in closer to Aladdin.

ABANAZER   There is a cave near here – a Cave of Wonders. The cave is filled with gold and silver, and every precious gem the world has ever imagined. Enough riches, I'll wager, to win the hand of your Princess.

ALADDIN   So, where is this cave? Why haven't you already been to get the gold?

ABANAZER	If only it were that simple. I'm not as fit as once I was. I need a young pair of legs and a strong back to go into the cave for me.
ALADDIN	And I can take all the jewels I want?
ABANAZER	As much as you can carry, young Aladdin.
ALADDIN	But, what about you? What do you get out of all this? You're already rich.
ABANAZER	There is a lamp, hidden deep within the cave. It is not of any real value, but it once belonged to my grandmother, and I'm a sentimental old fool.

He pulls Aladdin in closer.

ABANAZER	Fetch me the lamp, and the rest of the jewels are yours.
ALADDIN	But what's so special about an old lamp?

Abanazer tries to hold back his temper.

ABANAZER	Why you . . .! I have searched long and hard for this family heirloom. That is the only reward I desire.
ALADDIN	Then what are we waiting for?! Let's go find this cave!
ABANAZER	No need – we're already here!

Abanazer throws his hands into the air, and chants.

ABANAZER	By the powers of those who came before
	Open now this secret door
	Cave of Wonders, reveal to me
	And hear me shout – Open Sesame!

Lightning flashes across the sky as a rock moves away to reveal a narrow entrance down into the cave.

ABANAZER	Well, what are you waiting for? Get down there, and get me that lamp!
ALADDIN	But, it's very dark down there.
ABANAZER	You want to impress your Princess with all that gold, don't you?
ALADDIN	Yes, but . . .
ABANAZER	Well, get down there!

He gives Aladdin a shove with his foot. Aladdin takes a deep breath, and crawls through the tiny hole.

| ABANAZER | Hurry, boy. Hurry. |
| | *Lightning flashes. Blackout.* |

_____

Scene 10
Interior: Cave – Night

Aladdin makes his way through the dark, dank cave. The light of the tiny entrance can be seen shining from above.

Abanazer's voice echoes through the darkness.

ABANAZER	Hurry boy. The lamp.
ALADDIN	But uncle, where's all the gold? All the gems?
ABANAZER	Get me the lamp, and you'll get your reward!
ALADDIN	I'm scared, uncle. I'm coming out.
ABANAZER	You stupid boy! Bring me the lamp, or you'll never get out!
ALADDIN	Uncle . . . ?
ABANAZER	Haven't you worked it out yet, you imbecile?! I'm not your uncle. You don't have an uncle! Now bring me that lamp, or I shall seal this cave, and leave you to your doom!
ALADDIN	Never! You won't get your hands on any lamp until you tell me what's going on.
ABANAZER	Then on your own head be it! Once you have perished, another shall be able to enter the cave, and retrieve the lamp over your wasting bones. I shan't have to wait too long.

By those to whose power is strong and wild
Punish ye this stupid child
Trap him here eternally
By these words – Close Sesame!

Aladdin hurries to the door, but the light shuts off as the rock closes back over.

He's trapped.

ALADDIN	This is terrible. You idiot, Aladdin. All you had to do is find him that old lamp, and he'd have let you out. Now you're going to be trapped here forever.

He shivers.

ALADDIN	It's cold. I'm never going to see mum again, or Wishee, or Princess Blossom . . . I'm so stupid.

He wanders through the cave.

ALADDIN — I wonder if there's another way out.

A beam of light catches the lamp.

ALADDIN — Why, this must be the lamp he was talking about.

He picks it up.

ALADDIN — All that fuss for a battered up old lamp. He must be mad. Hey, I wonder if I can light the lamp? It might keep me warm for a while.

He starts to examine it closely.

ALADDIN — There's some writing here, but it's hidden by all the dust.

Aladdin starts to rub the lamp . . .

Suddenly, in a huge burst of light, the GENIE OF THE LAMP appears.

GENIE — Oh, is it good to be out of there!

The Genie spots Aladdin.

GENIE — Hey kid! You must be Aladdin, huh?

ALADDIN — Y . . .Yeah . . . How did you know?

GENIE — How did I know? I'm a genie, kid! I know everything! Plus, the word on the Genie grapevine is that you've been sort of destined to come here and rub the lamp. I was expecting you a lot sooner, but as you're here now . . .

The Genie bows.

GENIE — What can I get you, O Master?

ALADDIN — Now, wait a minute . . . How come you knew I was com . . . Did you just call me 'master'?

GENIE — Sure did, keeps up with the old master/servant role play. I like to keep it traditional.

ALADDIN — I'm your master?

GENIE — You got a sharp mind, kid, you're learning fast. You're my master, I'm the genie, and you got three wishes – as per the Genie rule book, code 27b, sub-clause 'a'.

ALADDIN — Three wishes?

GENIE	You're quicker than I thought. Why else would you be here?
ALADDIN	I came here because I was promised gold and gems, so that I could win the hand of a Princess.
GENIE	Oh, I love romantic stories. Is she beautiful?
ALADDIN	She's an angel!
GENIE	Bet she's clever, too, huh?
ALADDIN	You got it!
GENIE	And she can only marry a prince?

Aladdin's spirits drop.

ALADDIN	Yeah, she can only marry a prince.

The penny drops.

ALADDIN	Hey, wait a minute – she can only marry a prince!
GENIE	Oh, this is filling me up! So, this prince thing – is that an official wish?
ALADDIN	Uh, I suppose so.
GENIE	Ah-ah . . . You have to say it officially – sub-clause 'b'. Hey, I didn't write it . . .
ALADDIN	OK. Genie, I wish you to make me a prince!
GENIE	Sure! Anything else?
ALADDIN	Well, I wish you could get me out of this cave . . .
GENIE	That's wish number two. Hang on to your hat, kid!

MUSIC: GENIE'S SONG

As the Genie sings, the cave transforms. Spirits and dancers bring in caskets of gold and jewels, and tailors change Aladdin's rags for prince's robes.

At the end of the song, the Cave of Wonders is filled with every jewel and gem imaginable.

Blackout.

End of ACT ONE

————————————————

ACT TWO

Scene 1
Exterior: Street – Day

Abanazer wanders through the stalls, laughing evilly.

ABANAZER That fool Aladdin! He thinks he can get the better of me . . . Well, a couple of days sealed in that dark cave ought to change his mind. He'll be clamouring to give me the lamp, then.

He laughs again, and gazes around the audience.

ABANAZER Children, children, everywhere – and not a one to eat. You little brats! You thought you'd got the better of me with your hissing and your booing – but look at me now, eh?! Within a matter of days, I shall control the world. And, I poisoned all your sweets!

More boos and hisses!

ABANAZER Oh, you can boo all you like! When I'm in charge, homework will be doubled! There'll be no more telly! And everyone will be forced to eat sprouts and cabbage for tea!

More laughter as he reaches the stage.

The Slave appears again. This time he's dressed up to the nines.

ABANAZER What are you doing here? I didn't summon you!
SLAVE Ooh, get him . . . No, I'm just on my way out for the Magical Assistant of the Year Awards, but I thought you'd like to know that things aren't quite as rosy as you hope they are.
ABANAZER What do you mean?
SLAVE Aladdin has used the lamp!
ABANAZER What?!
SLAVE He's summoned the Genie, and turned himself into a prince! He's on his way back to Pekin now.
ABANAZER How do you know all of this?
SLAVE The Genie of the Lamp is my second cousin . . .

He whips out a mobile 'phone.

SLAVE And it's good to talk! Byee!

Making a Drama out of a Crisis   *Aladdin* **script**

36

	In another puff of smoke, he's gone.
ABANAZER	That idiot Aladdin! How dare he use my lamp?! Well, I'll show him . . . I'll get the lamp back, and have my revenge. Where are those two stupid policemen? Chop! Suey!
	Chop and Suey stumble onto the stage.
CHOP and SUEY	Yes, Chief Inspector?
ABANAZER	Oh, stop it with this wooden 'yes, Chief Inspector' nonsense – you're under my control, not auditioning for Hollyoaks!
	They revert back to their normal voices.
CHOP	Oh, OK.
SUEY	Right you are.
	Abanazer huddles in to Chop and Suey.
ABANAZER	Aladdin has returned, and he's got the lamp. I must find where he keeps it, and get it back.
	Chop and Suey stare at him blankly. Abanazer tries again.
ABANAZER	I need to find the lamp, and get it from him.
CHOP	So you said.
SUEY	I heard him too.
ABANAZER	You fools! I want you to find out where he keeps the lamp, and I want to steal it from him!
CHOP	Oh, well why didn't you say so?
SUEY	Steal it from him? Isn't stealing against the law?
CHOP	Oh, it is. We couldn't possibly be caught stealing. We'd have to throw ourselves in jail.
SUEY	And throw away our key.
	Abanazer tries to control his mood.
ABANAZER	Then go in disguise! And make it a clever one. You'll have to mingle in the background, so that no one will see you.
CHOP	A disguise. That's clever that.
SUEY	It is, really clever.
	Abanazer shouts.
ABANAZER	Well, get on with it then!
	Chop and Suey both salute, and march off together. Abanazer shakes his head, and follows.

Scene 2
Interior: Twankey's Laundry – Day

Twankey and Wishee are doing the laundry in silence, both very upset.

TWANKEY	I can't believe that my poor little boy has been executed!
WISHEE	Come on, mum – don't get upset again.
TWANKEY	But it's Christmas, and my poor little Aladdin's gone and lost his head. I'll have to take his Christmas presents back and change them.
WISHEE	Mum, Aladdin's had his head chopped off! What are you going to change his presents for?
TWANKEY	Well, I could get him a flat cap, a pair of sunglasses, a pipe . . . Oooh . . .!

She starts to cry again.

WISHEE	Come on, mum. We have to remember the good times. Aladdin was handsome . . .
TWANKEY	Yes, he was.
WISHEE	He was courageous . . .
TWANKEY	Yes, he was.
WISHEE	He was a romantic . . .
TWANKEY	Yes, he was.
WISHEE	He just should have quit while he was ahead.
TWANKEY	Ooooh . . .!

Twankey cries again. She pulls a big pair of bloomers from a laundry basket, and blows her nose on them.

TWANKEY	There's something I never told you, Wishee.
WISHEE	What's that mum?
TWANKEY	Aladdin was adopted.
WISHEE	Adopted?
TWANKEY	Yes. I found him in a laundry basket lying in the gutter, abandoned.
WISHEE	Lying in the gutter?
TWANKEY	Yes, your father wanted to call him Dwayne.
WISHEE	And you took him in as your own?

Twankey nods, and blows her nose again.

TWANKEY   All he had in the world was this golden medallion around his neck . . .

ALADDIN (O.S.) You mean like this one?

They look up to see Aladdin enter, dressed in fine clothes, and followed by servants carrying trays of gold and gems.

WISHEE   Aladdin! You're alive!

ALADDIN   Yes, and no thanks to that no good 'uncle' of ours. He's not our uncle at all – just some lunatic out to take over the world.

TWANKEY   Oh, Aladdin – you're alive, you're safe, you've won the lottery . . .

ALADDIN   Not the lottery, mum – but I have got this.

He pulls out the lamp, and gives it a rub. The Genie enters.

GENIE   Hey, big Al! Good to see you again. Dig the sharp look, man. Why you're even better lookin' than the last time I saw you.

Aladdin blushes.

ALADDIN   Good, innit?

Twankey wanders over to the Genie.

TWANKEY   Well, hello there. Where have you been all my life?

GENIE   Well, I wasn't born for most of it . . .

ALADDIN   Mum, Wishee – meet the Genie of the Lamp!

The Genie bows deeply.

TWANKEY   A genie? You mean, all this is real?! I'm not dreaming?

ALADDIN   No mum, you're not dreaming. We're rich!

               MUSIC: CELEBRATION SONG

During the song, spirits dress Wishee and Twankey in rich outfits. At the end, everyone exits happily.

Scene 3
Interior: Palace – Day

Abanazer enters the empty throne room.

ABANAZER   Oh, shut up!

He looks around for Chop and Suey.

ABANAZER   Where are those two imbeciles? I told them to be here
                before the Emperor arrives, and in disguise.

SUEY (O.S.)   Here we are!

                MUSIC: *STAR WARS* THEME

*Chop and Suey rush on dressed as Yoda and Darth Vader.
They're battling with light sabres.*

Chop, as Vader, stops and 'feels' a disturbance in the force.

CHOP   Today is Luke Skywalker's birthday. He is getting a
                Playstation, a remote control car, and an action man.

SUEY   How can you tell?

CHOP   I have felt his presents.

They battle again. Abanazer stops them.

ABANAZER   What are you two imbeciles doing?

Suey answers as Yoda.

SUEY   Mmm, in disguise, we are.

ABANAZER   What sort of disguises to you call these?

SUEY   Mmm, good disguises, they are.

ABANAZER   But I told you to get disguises that would help you blend
                into the background.

SUEY   Mmm, run out, the shop had.

Abanazer slaps him across his head.

ABANAZER   Stop talking like that!

Chop lifts his light sabre threateningly.

CHOP   The force is strong with you, old man – but you cannot
                stop me, for I am . . . I am . . .

SUEY   Luke's father?

CHOP   No . . . I am . . .

Making a Drama out of a Crisis   *Aladdin* script

40

He lifts his cape to reveal a pair of pink, fluffy bunny slippers, and sings.

CHOP I am what I am
And what I am, needs no excuses . . .

ABANAZER Stop it, the pair of you. Now the Princess and the Emperor will be here any minute . . .

SUEY Emperor Palpatine has captured Princess Amidala?

Abanazer puts his arm around Suey, and leads him gently downstage.

ABANAZER Tell me . . . what did Father Christmas bring you?

SUEY Oh, I got a Steps CD, a book all about dinosaurs, and a new pair of stabilizers for my bike.

Abanazer nods.

ABANAZER If you make one more stupid *Star Wars* comment, you'll be sending Father Christmas an urgent fax, asking him to come back, and swap all your presents for a new set of teeth. Do I make myself very, very clear?

Suey nods slowly.

SUEY Yep.

ABANAZER Good. Shall we continue?

SUEY OK.

Abanazer and Suey get back into position.

ABANAZER In a few moments' time, Princess Blossom and her father will be here to receive Aladdin, dressed as Prince Ali. He will ask for the Princess's hand in marriage, and the Emperor will most likely say yes. However, while all this is going on, you will be hidden here in this room, trying to grab the lamp which Aladdin will be carrying with him. Is that understood?

Chop and Suey nod blankly.

ABANAZER Oh, why couldn't I have been in Cinderella again like last year?

He hears a noise.

ABANAZER Right, they're coming. Hide!

Making a Drama out of a Crisis *Aladdin* **script**

Chop hides behind a tapestry hanging on the wall, and Suey conceals himself behind the Emperor's throne.

Chop's light sabre is sticking out from behind the tapestry. Abanazer slaps it hard, and Chop pulls it away.

ABANAZER   Imbeciles!

He exits quickly.

The Emperor and his court enter, followed by the Princess, Aladdin, Wishee Washee, and Widow Twankey, dressed in an outrageous outfit.

The Emperor sits on his throne. As Aladdin passes, Suey makes a grab for the lamp, hanging from his belt. The Emperor stands on his hand, forcing him to stifle his cry.

ALADDIN   Your Majesty, I, Prince Ali, have come here today to ask for the hand in marriage of your daughter, Princess Blossom.

Wishee whispers in his ear.

ALADDIN   Oh yes, and for the hand of the Princess's lady-in-waiting, Daisy, for my brother, The Duke of Washee.

Daisy giggles, and hides behind a fan.

Chop tries to grab the lamp as Aladdin passes again. No luck.

EMPEROR   Well, this is all very exciting, isn't it? You're a very impressive youth, and prince to boot. Because, as we all know – only a prince can marry a princess.

Suey reaches out from beneath the throne, fondling wildly for the lamp. He is unnoticed.

The Emperor turns to Princess Blossom.

EMPEROR   Well, what do you say, my dear?

The Princess smiles at Aladdin.

BLOSSOM   I say yes, father.

EMPEROR   Very well, it is arranged. Two days from now – we shall have a royal wedding.

The court cheers and congratulates Aladdin and Blossom. Chop and Suey both reach out, and grab the wrong people.

TWANKEY	Ooh, good. I do like a good knees up.
	The Emperor spots Twankey, and smiles. He gets up off his throne and approaches her.
EMPEROR	Well, what do we have here?
	Twankey pulls out a huge fan to hide behind.
EMPEROR	And what is your name, my dear?
TWANKEY	Dame Twankey of Piddle.
EMPEROR	Piddle?
TWANKEY	Yes, it's the name of the village I was born in. There's Upper Piddle where the shops are, and Lower Piddle, where the river was – but I lived somewhere between the two.
EMPEROR	Where was that?
TWANKEY	Middle Piddle.
	The Emperor notices that Aladdin and Blossom are holding hands and gazing into each other's eyes.
EMPEROR	I think we'd better leave our love birds alone.
	He gestures for the members of his court to leave. They offer their congratulations to Aladdin and Blossom as they go. Even Suey joins the line-up to shake their hands.
SUEY	I do love a royal wedding.
	Chop grabs him, and pulls him off stage.
	Aladdin and Blossom are left alone together.
BLOSSOM	Well, it's really happening.
ALADDIN	Yes.
BLOSSOM	I'm really getting married to a prince.
ALADDIN	Yes.
BLOSSOM	And now you can teach me to climb the great oak.
ALADDIN	Ye . . . er . . . I don't know what you're talking about.
BLOSSOM	I know it's you Aladdin. This Prince Ali stuff doesn't fool me.
ALADDIN	If you know I'm not a real prince, does that mean we can't get married?
BLOSSOM	Not as long as father still thinks you're a prince – and you'll always be a prince to me.

MUSIC: LOVE SONG

At the end of the song, Aladdin and Princess Blossom exit, holding hands.

Scene 4
Exterior: Palace – Day

Abanazer enters, not a happy man.

ABANAZER   If you want something done properly, get rid of the bumbling policemen before you start!

He strides about the stage.

ABANAZER   So, Aladdin still has the lamp, and now he's getting married to the Princess. Yuk! It's enough to make a grown man sick. I have to get that lamp! But how . . . how?

The Slave appears – he's obviously been disturbed as he's holding a champagne bottle, and kissing the air.

SLAVE   Mmmmwah! Oh, it's you. I was just in the middle of something . . .

He leans over, and shouts into the ring.

SLAVE   I won't be long . . . I'm just popping into something more comfortable.

To Abanazer.

SLAVE   Can we make this quick? I have company.

ABANAZER   So I see. How on Earth is there enough room for two of you in there?

SLAVE   Well, there isn't really – you have to squeeze up close . . . Now, what do you want?

ABANAZER   I'll let your attitude go this time, as I need your help. Aladdin still has the lamp, and those two brainless bobbies couldn't get it back.

SLAVE   I told you, it's no use getting all worked up about that old thing.

ABANAZER   The lamp, you say it's old?

SLAVE   Oooh, I'll say. Been in the family for generations.

ABANAZER   And dirty, too?

SLAVE   Filthy. I wouldn't give it house room.

ABANAZER   That's it!

SLAVE   What's it?

Making a Drama out of a Crisis   *Aladdin* script

ABANAZER	My plan! If the lamp is old and dirty, then why wouldn't they want to swap it for a nice, shiny new one? It would make a wonderful wedding present, and it'd be more of a conversation piece than some toaster from Argos . . .
SLAVE	Oh, you've lost it this time. Can I go now, and leave you to your delusions. I do have someone waiting . . .
ABANAZER	Yes, yes, begone.
SLAVE	Charming!

The Slave exits

ABANAZER	Delusions indeed . . . My plan is formed. I shall disguise myself cunningly, and offer them a deal they cannot refuse. Just a few more hours – and the lamp will be mine.

He laughs wickedly again as he exits.

_____

Scene 5
Exterior: Palace Gardens – Evening

Widow Twankey, Princess Blossom and her ladies-in-waiting are preparing for the wedding.

Wishee Washee is with them in regimental uniform.
Twankey tries to get his sword to hang straight

TWANKEY | Will you keep still, Wishee? I can't get your sword to hang right.

WISHEE | Oh, do I have to wear this, mum? I forgot about it before, sat down quick and before I knew it I'd cut three of my toenails.

TWANKEY | Now, you be quiet. It's not every day both of my sons get married. Besides, he looks very smart, doesn't he girls?

The Princess and the girls nod.

DAISY | I think you look very handsome.

Wishee blushes and hides behind Twankey.

BLOSSOM | Dame Twankey, when Aladdin and I get married tomorrow, does that mean I can call you mum?

Twankey smiles, sweetly.

TWANKEY | Of course you can, love. You'll be my young Princess, and I'll be your . . .

WISHEE | Old Queen.

Twankey slaps Wishee across the head again

TWANKEY | Right, come on then girls, let's try on those bridesmaids dresses, and Daisy's bridal gown.

Wishee blushes again.

TWANKEY | And we'd best get you a cork for the end of that before you put someone's eye out with it.

Twankey leads Rose, Daisy, and Wishee off stage. Blossom stays on, putting together flowers for her bouquet.

Abanazer enters, hunched up under a beggar's cowl. He speaks in an old man's voice.

ABANAZER	New lamps for old . . . new lamps for old.
	He hears the audience hissing him, and briefly looks up from beneath his disguise.
ABANAZER	Shut up, the lot of you, or I'll pinch your presents.
	He heads over to the Princess.
ABANAZER	New lamps for old . . . new lamps for old . . .
BLOSSOM	What's that you say, old man?
ABANAZER	I'm a poor old man, trying to eke my way through life by trading in old, dirty lamps for bright, shiny new ones.
BLOSSOM	You take old lamps, and give new ones in return?
ABANAZER	You catch on fast, young lady. Er . . ., would you happen to have any old, dusty lamps lying around that you would like to replace?
BLOSSOM	No thank you, old man – we're very happy with our lamps.
	She goes back to making her bouquet. Abanazer pulls a shining golden lamp from beneath his cowl.
ABANAZER	But look how my new lamps glisten . . .
BLOSSOM	That is an impressive lamp. But why do you give them out, and take the old worthless lamps away?
ABANAZER	I'm a poor old man, I take them down to the *Antiques Roadshow* to try and make a penny or two.
BLOSSOM	Well, Aladdin does have a dusty old lamp that he carries around with him.
	She searches beneath the bench, and pulls out the lamp.
BLOSSOM	But, he's away trying on his wedding outfit, so I couldn't really exchange it without his permission.
	Abanazer's eyes are bright with greed at the sight of the lamp.
ABANAZER	But, imagine his joy when he finds the new lamp in its place.
BLOSSOM	I'm not sure . . .
ABANAZER	You say you're getting married . . . What better wedding present to give your new husband than a new, shiny lamp?
	Blossom turns Aladdin's lamp over in her hands.

BLOSSOM	I don't know. Aladdin does seem very attached to this old thing. Should I do it boys and girls? Should I change this old lamp for a nice new one?

The audience shout 'no!'

Abanazer tries to shout over them.

ABANAZER	I am a very poor man, I have not eaten in a long time. That lamp could fetch me enough to buy a loaf of stale bread . . .
BLOSSOM	What do you think, boys and girls . . .?

'No!'

ABANAZER	I have children to feed. Six . . . teen of them.
BLOSSOM	Sixteen children?
ABANAZER	Yes, and I'm saving to pay for my sister's eye operation. She's having another glass eye put in.
BLOSSOM	*Another* glass eye?
ABANAZER	Yes, she's always wanted the matching pair.
BLOSSOM	Two glass eyes? How does she see?
ABANAZER	Not very well at all. Now will you swap the lamp?
BLOSSOM	I don't know. Maybe if I polished it up a bit, you might get a bit more money for it . . .

She makes to rub the lamp. Abanazer shouts out

ABANAZER	No, don't rub it!

He reverts back to his old man persona.

ABANAZER	I mean, please don't rub it, young miss. I wouldn't want to dirty those pretty little hands of yours.
BLOSSOM	Well, that's very kind of you. You seem like a very nice old man, so I will swap this lamp for your new one.

Abanazer reaches out with trembling hands and takes the lamp. With a joyous yell, he casts off his disguise, and holds the lamp above his head.

ABANAZER	Yes! I have it at last! The lamp that will bring to me eternal power.

Blossom cowers back in fear.

ABANAZER	I must thank you Princess, you have bestowed an extraordinary gift upon me. You will not be forgotten for this.

Suddenly Aladdin, Twankey and Wishee rush on

ALADDIN	Princess, is everything alright? I heard a cry!
ABANAZER	Well, if it isn't His Most Royal Highness Prince Ali . . . Or should I say Aladdin, the son of a humble washerwoman.
TWANKEY	You watch your mouth.
ALADDIN	Abanazer, I might have known it was you.

Abanazer mimics him.

ABANAZER	'I might have known it was you'. Soon the whole world shall know my name, and the whole world will bow down before me – Abanazer, the greatest wizard of them all!

He laughs evilly again, and starts to leave.

ALADDIN	Not so fast, Abanazer.

He draws his regimental sword from his wedding outfit.

ALADDIN	I won't let you get away without a fight.

He leaps up onto the bench, sword held high.

Abanazer grabs Princess Blossom, and holds her against him as a shield.

ABANAZER	How very brave, and how very, very foolish. Would you harm your Princess to get to me? I think not. I depart now for my secret lair where my plans for world domination shall unfold.
ALADDIN	You let her go! This is between you and me!
ABANAZER	I don't think so.

He holds the Princess tighter.

ABANAZER	Now Princess, I hope you don't get airsick, because we're going for a little ride on my magic carpet – and I haven't even got permission to fly through Chinese airspace.

Abanazer clutches the lamp tightly, and drags Princess Blossom off stage

TWANKEY	Oh no, what are we going to do?

ALADDIN	I have to go after her!
WISHEE	But how? He has a magic carpet, and we don't even know where he's headed.
TWANKEY	Oh, look – the poor dear's even lost her engagement ring.

Twankey stoops to pick up Abanazer's ring from the floor. Aladdin takes it.

ALADDIN	That isn't the Princess's ring, it's Abanazer's. I saw him wearing it in the laundry. He must have dropped it.
TWANKEY	Well, he doesn't look after it very well.

Twankey rubs the ring, and the Slave appears, dressed in his pyjamas and carrying a hot water bottle

SLAVE	Oh, will you stop that! I was getting an early night . . . Wait a minute, you're not Abanazer!
ALADDIN	No, I'm Aladdin. Abanazer has kidnapped the Princess, and he's taking her to his secret lair on a magic carpet.
SLAVE	Kidnapped the Princess? Ooh, he's gone too far this time!
ALADDIN	Can you help us find his secret lair?
SLAVE	Find it? Who do you think chose it? He would have settled for a two-bedroom flat in Gateshead if it wasn't for me pushing him to look around.
ALADDIN	But how do we get there?
SLAVE	Oh, that's easy! Have you ever flown a magic carpet before?

Aladdin shakes his head.

SLAVE	Well, it's quite simple, but the in-flight meal isn't up to much. I'd take a nice packed lunch if I were you.

Aladdin turns to Wishee.

ALADDIN	Tell the Emperor to call out the police, and follow us. We'll need all the help we can get.

He sheathes his sword and faces the Slave

ALADDIN	Right, we're ready.

The Slave waves his hot water bottle in the air. The lights flash.

Blackout

Scene 6
Exterior: Sky – Night

MUSIC: FUNNY MUSIC

Abanazer and the Princess are seen sweeping through the night sky on a flying carpet. (They are running with carpets around their waists, and black-clad legs. False legs hang over the edge of the carpet to give the impression of flying.)

The Princess is struggling against Abanazer, but grips the edge of the carpet tightly.

Other carpets follow: Aladdin pushing his carpet to go faster, Wishee being dragged behind his carpet, Chop and Suey with a blue flashing light on their carpet, the Emperor on a royal golden carpet, and Twankey on a large 'Welcome' mat.

The carpets chase each other around the stage, getting into each other's way, and almost colliding on several occasions.

Eventually – blackout.

The lights come up to reveal . . .

Scene 7
Interior: Abanazer's Lair – Night

Abanazer's lair is the inside of a pyramid tomb.

Abanazer rushes in, and throws the Princess to the floor. He stands in the centre of the tomb, and raises the lamp above his head

ABANAZER   Make yourself comfortable, Princess – I have to take over the world.

That maniacal laugh again as he rubs the lamp. In a puff of smoke, the Genie appears.

GENIE   Just give that lamp a little rub, and I'll pop out to help ya, Bub . . . Hey Al, you look kinda different. Did you get a haircut?

ABANAZER   Silence, you imbecile! Why, you're as stupid as that idiotic Slave of the Ring!

GENIE   Hey, now something tells me that you're not Al, and you leave my second cousin out of this.

ABANAZER   I shall enjoy commanding you . . .

ALADDIN (*O.S.*)   Not so fast, Abanazer!

Aladdin runs on, followed by Wishee, Twankey, the Emperor, and Chop and Suey.

TWANKEY   Ooh, this place could do with a visit from *Changing Rooms* . . .

ABANAZER   Well, well, well . . . if it isn't the Spice Girls. Do your worst, Aladdin – in a few moments, you shall bow down before my feet.

ALADDIN   Let the Princess go. This has nothing to do with her.

ABANAZER   Oh, I couldn't possibly do that. For when I'm King of the World, I shall need a Queen. Princess Blossom will marry me!

ALADDIN   Not until I have spent my last breath!

Aladdin draws his sword and charges at Abanazer. He grabs a sword from the tomb, and fights back.

MUSIC: EXCITING MUSIC

A thrilling duel commences as Aladdin and Abanazer fight back and forth around the stage.

Princess Blossom runs over to Twankey, who comforts her.

ALADDIN   You'll rule the world over my dead body, Abanazer.

ABANAZER   How kind of you to offer . . .

Eventually, Aladdin spins Abanazer's sword away, and backs him up against the edge of the tomb.

ABANAZER   Do your worst Aladdin . . . only make it good, because if you leave me be, I shall be back to fight another day.

EMPEROR   Chop, Suey – seize him!

ABANAZER   I don't think so. Not while they're under my control.

GENIE   They're under your control? Not any more . . .

The Genie snaps his fingers, and Chop and Suey come out of their trance. They seem a little disoriented for a second.

SUEY   Ooh, 'eck! Where are we?

CHOP   Remind me never to let you buy the drinks again.

EMPEROR   Sergeant . . .

Chop and Suey take Abanazer by the arms, and hold him.

Aladdin turns to the audience.

ALADDIN   What shall I do with him gang?

The audience shout out all manner of horrific punishments.

ALADDIN   I've got a better idea. Genie, if he rubbed the lamp, is he your master now?

GENIE   No way, Al. Until he makes his first wish, you're still my master, dude!

ABANAZER   In that case, I wi . . .

Suey clamps a hand over his mouth.

SUEY   I wouldn't . . . Not unless you want to send an urgent fax to Father Christmas asking for a new set of teeth . . .

ALADDIN   And how many wishes have I used up?

GENIE   That would be two, my man – one to get you out of the cave, and one to make you a prince.

Making a Drama out of a Crisis   *Aladdin* script

ALADDIN	And if I use my third to make Abanazer behave?
GENIE	I'm afraid you won't be a prince anymore, Al. You won't be able to marry the Princess.

Aladdin approaches the Princess and holds her hands.

ALADDIN	I love you with all my heart, but I can't let Abanazer go to ruin other people's lives.
BLOSSOM	I understand . . .
TWANKEY	Ooh, I'm filling up . . .!

Aladdin kisses Blossom gently, then turns to the Genie.

ALADDIN	Genie, for my final wish – I wish for Abanazer to always be kind and good.
GENIE	Consider it done, pal!

The Genie swaps Aladdin's rich clothes for his ragged waistcoat. Abanazer is simpering, and handing out flowers to everyone.

ABANAZER	There's one for you, and one for you . . . oh, you're all such beautiful people. I'm going to have a tea party on Saturday for all my friends, and you're all invited!

He grins inanely.

SUEY	I think I preferred him when he was bad.

Chop sneezes loudly into his flower.

CHOP	It was better for my hay fever.

Aladdin takes the Princess's hand.

ALADDIN	Now I'm not a prince, I can't marry you. I'm not even supposed to look upon your face.

He takes off his golden amulet, and hands it to her.

ALADDIN	I want you to have this, so you will always remember me.
BLOSSOM	I could never forget you, my sweet prince. It's beautiful.
EMPEROR	It certainly is. Where did you get this, young man?
ALADDIN	I . . . I don't know. I've always had it.
EMPEROR	This is the royal seal of Istanbul. This was given to their lost Prince on the day he was saved from an evil revolution.

Twankey steps forward.

TWANKEY	It was around his neck on the day I found him.
ALADDIN	You found me?
TWANKEY	Yes Aladdin, I found you and adopted you. I didn't know how to tell you.
EMPEROR	You know what this means? The boy is the lost heir to the throne. He is a genuine prince after all!
ALADDIN	You mean . . . the wedding can still go ahead?
EMPEROR	My little Princess has found her prince again. I don't see why not.
ABANAZER	Oh, goodie. Can I be bridesmaid?

Suey clamps a hand over his mouth again.

TWANKEY	Well, if Aladdin and Blossom are getting married, and Wishee Washee's still getting wed to Daisy – how do you fancy making it a triple wedding? I quite fancy being an Empress . . .
EMPEROR	Well, you are an expert at laundry, and I could do with someone to iron my shirts.
TWANKEY	In the interests of marital bliss, I'll pretend I didn't hear that.

Aladdin and Princess Blossom exit as everyone congratulates them.

End of ACT TWO

FINALE

Scene 1
Interior: Palace – Day

MUSIC: FINALE MUSIC

The characters walk down to take their bows:

Dancers and spirits
Townsfolk and policemen
Rose and Pansy
The Slave and Genie
The Emperor
Chop and Suey
Wishee Washee and Daisy
Abanazer
Widow Twankey
Aladdin and Princess Blossom.
Chancellor
Voice (of Sphinx)

MUSIC: FINAL SONG

At the end of the song, the cast close the show with a traditional pantomime rhyme!

WISHEE	And so our tale is at an end We hope it made you smile.
SLAVE	And dream of far-off places.
GENIE	And adventures for a while.
Chop	A land of myth and magic.
SUEY	And laughs aplenty, too.
EMPEROR	Where a pair of star-crossed lovers Fell in love, as lovers do.
ABANAZER	A place where good will triumph And the bad will pay their price.
BLOSSOM	A land where wishes can come true.
ALADDIN	Not once, or twice, but thrice.

TWANKEY	And so we bid you all farewell
	And leave you full of cheer.
ALL	So have a Merry Christmas
	And a wonderful New Year!

(Panto is for life – not just for Christmas – so feel free to adapt the final two lines if you're performing at any other time of year!)

THE END

Remember this entire script can be downloaded from the Continuum Books website, ready for you to load into your word processor and trim where necessary. Just go to:

www.continuumbooks.com/resources/9781855394469

Index

Index